AMERICAN RIGHTS

LEGAL RIGHTS

TERRY JOHNSON

Facts On File, Inc.

Legal Rights

Facts On File, Inc.
An imprint of Infobase Publishing
132 West 31st Street
New York NY 10001

ISBN-10: 0-8160-5665-X
ISBN-13: 978-0-8160-5665-1

Library of Congress Cataloging-in-Publication Data
  Johnson, Terry, 1961–
  Legal rights / Terry Johnson.
        p. cm.—(American rights)
  Includes bibliographical references and index.
  ISBN 0-8160-5665-X (alk. paper)
  1. Civil rights—United States. 2. Civil rights—United States—History. I. Title.
  II. Series.
  KF4749.J64 2005
  342.7308'5—dc22   2004023350

Text design by Erika K. Arroyo
Cover design by Pehrsson Design
Maps and graphs by Sholto Ainslie

Printed in the United States of America

VB FOF 10 9 8 7 6 5 4 3 2

This book is printed on acid-free paper.

Contents

Introduction

American Legal Rights

The First Amendment of the Bill of Rights promises that the U.S. Congress cannot, by law, take away the freedom of people to speak their minds, to practice a religion, to join a peaceful political group, or to publish a newspaper. For people to feel safe enough to enjoy these rights, the government must be powerful enough to protect the country and the people in it. On the other hand, if a government has unlimited power to inspire fear and use force, any bill of rights could easily become meaningless. In decisions regarding the Fourth through Eighth Amendments, the U.S. Supreme Court, throughout its history, has had to balance two concerns: Allowing the government enough power to maintain security, and limiting the government's power enough to protect people from its abuse.

In fact, the government is quite powerful. To protect individuals and the country from criminals, terrorists, and enemy countries, the government can search people's homes, read people's personal e-mails and private letters, secretly watch people, listen in on their private conversations, and take people's property. And, as computers and other electronic devices become more advanced, the government becomes even more able to search and spy. By law, the government (and only the government) can put people on trial for crimes and punish those found guilty, in some cases by putting them to death.

The rights guaranteed in the Fourth through Eighth Amendments limit the power of the government to do these things and help ensure that the government carries out the law fairly. People have, among other rights, the right not to be searched or arrested, and the right not to have their property searched or taken, without a good legal reason; the right not to confess or be witnesses against themselves; the right to be treated fairly; the right to trial by jury; the right to a speedy and public trial; the right to call and question witnesses; and the right against excessive, cruel, and unusual punishments.

After the terrorist attacks of September 11, 2001, the government quickly expanded its power in order to hunt down the terrorists and to prevent future terrorist attacks. Without delay, law enforcement officers began seizing people who the government suspected were terrorists or had ties to terrorism. Two months after the attacks, the government had seized more than 1,200 citizens and noncitizens living in the United States. Many of those seized were later arrested. Most of those held were Muslim men from Arab countries. (All of the September 11 terrorists were from the Middle East.)

Nearly a month after the attacks, the United States and its ally Great Britain began attacking Afghanistan, the country harboring the terrorist group that planned the attacks. After the war, the United States transferred captured enemy fighters to its U.S. naval base at Guantánamo Bay, Cuba. The United States also captured American citizens who were fighting with the enemy and transferred these fighters to prisons in the United States.

U.S. president George W. Bush declared that the prisoners at Guantánamo—especially those the government believes are terrorists—do not have the same rights, such as the right not to be tortured, as those held by traditional prisoners of war. The government also claimed that prisoners in the United States who the government suspects are terrorists or have ties to terrorism do not have the right to see a lawyer or other rights normally held by those suspected of committing crimes.

The U.S. Congress also moved quickly to increase the government's power to protect the country against terrorism. In the month after the terrorist attacks, Congress passed the USA PATRIOT Act. The act's title is short for "Uniting and Strengthening America by Providing Appropriate Tools Required to Intercept and Obstruct Terrorism." The government now has more power to spy on people within and outside the United States, to hold and remove from the country noncitizens suspected of being terrorists or of having ties to terrorism, to prevent foreigners suspected of being terrorists from entering the country, and to do other things to prevent future terrorist attacks. Some (including the president and his advisers) believe that the government needs even more power to fight terrorism.

Others, however, have become concerned that the government has limited the freedom of citizens and noncitizens too much for the sake of security. Some groups and family members of prisoners have brought court cases to limit the government's increased power. In *Hamdi v. Rumsfeld* (2004), the U.S. Supreme Court said that U.S. citizens who are "enemy combatants" have certain rights that other prisoners have under the Fifth Amendment. In *Rasul v. Bush* (2004), the Court said that people speaking on behalf of foreign prisoners at Guantánamo Bay can ask a U.S. court to decide whether the federal government has imprisoned them illegally. As other cases make their way through the courts, the Court will probably have to judge whether the government's expanded power threatens other rights under the Fourth through Eighth Amendments.

Origins of American Legal Rights

When settlers from England arrived on the Atlantic seaboard of North America beginning in the early 17th century, they brought with them all of the traditional rights of English people. The colonists knew this because their charters (documents granting the settlers the power to set up their colonies) said so. For instance, the Virginia Charter of 1606, the first royal charter to set up a permanent English settlement in America, said that the colonists of Virginia were to "Have and enjoy all [rights and liberties] to all Intents and Purposes, as if they had been abiding and born, within this our Realm of England." Colonial charters, however, did not say in detail what these rights were.

In England's view, however, the American colonists enjoyed these rights not by right but by grace: The monarch (the ruling king or queen) could change or cancel these charters at will. By law, the colonies were under the total control of the monarch. Thus, in theory, the monarch could govern them directly according to his or her judgment, without regard to English law. In the end, the refusal of the Americans to accept that their rights were at the monarch's mercy led them to rebel and declare independence from Great Britain in 1776. (Scotland and England united to become Great Britain in 1707.) Years after the American Revolution, the Americans further protected these rights by creating the Bill of Rights.

When the first English settlers landed in America, much of what the English people considered to be their rights was based on common law, a body of law based on custom and the decisions of earlier judges. English common law developed over the centuries from the decisions of English royal courts established during the 13th century. By the time the American colonists formally declared their independence from Britain in 1776, they considered the common law rights guaranteed by Magna Carta of 1215, the Petition of Right of 1628, and the English Bill of Rights of 1689 to be a birthright. These English documents are the basis of English constitutional rights and are forerunners of the American Bill of Rights.

MAGNA CARTA
(1215)

The most famous charter is Magna Carta (also Magna Charta) of 1215. "Magna Carta" is a Latin phrase meaning "Great Charter." Magna Carta was originally an agreement between England's king John (who ruled from 1199 to 1216) and his barons. (A *baron* was a man who pledged his loyalty and service to a superior, such as a monarch, in return for land he could pass to his heirs, those who could receive the land by legal right at the baron's death. A woman who received land under the same conditions was called a *baroness*). In time, however, the English people (including the American colonists) saw Magna Carta as the source of English constitutional rights.

To finance his failed wars with France, King John had raised taxes, obtained money by force or threats from the barons and the towns, and taken properties. Henry II and Richard I, the two previous kings, had also violated the barons' rights and privileges. The barons rebelled against John. In 1215, the barons wrote a charter of liberties and sent it to the king. John refused to stamp the charter with the royal seal (wax stamped with the king's mark), which would have shown that he approved the charter. When he refused to seal the charter, the barons withdrew their loyalty to John. In May 1215, the barons marched on London and took the city. On June 15, John met the barons at Runnymede, a meadow, and sealed the charter, now known as Magna Carta.

At the time, the barons were concerned with their own interests. Nevertheless, many of the barons' demands had importance far beyond the barons' own direct interests. In fact, the charter (originally written in Latin) declared that the rights guaranteed by it are "granted to all freemen of our kingdom, for us and our heirs forever." (A *freeman* or *free man* is someone who has the full rights of a citizen.) Magna Carta was reissued with changes in 1216 (after John's death), 1217, and 1225. The 1225 version was put into English statute law in 1297. (Statutes are laws passed by a legislature, a government's body of lawmakers.) By the end of the 14th century, Magna Carta had become more than a statute: It had become (such as a country's constitution) fundamental law, a basic body of laws and principles superior to statutes and other laws.

During the 17th century, Magna Carta was a rallying cry for the English Parliament (England's congress) and its supporters in that body's battle against the tyranny (dictator-like rule) of the Stuart kings (James I, his son Charles I, and Charles's sons Charles II and James II). The Stuart kings ruled England from 1603 to 1649, and from 1660 to 1714. Sir Edward Coke (pronounced "Cook"), an important legal thinker and an outspoken critic of the abuses of the Stuart kings when he was speaker of the House of Commons, claimed that no monarch could violate rights guaranteed by Magna Carta, including the right against being arrested without legal reasons. (The British Parliament's House of Commons is similar to the House of Representatives in the U.S. Congress; like the speaker of the House of Representatives, the speaker directs the House of Commons during sessions.)

English people who settled in America during the 17th century brought the principles of Magna Carta with them. For example, William Penn, the founder of Pennsylvania, used Magna Carta as a source when he wrote the new colony's Frame of Government in 1682. Also, several colonies restated chapter 39 of Magna Carta in their laws and charters. Chapter 39 says, "No freemen shall be captured or imprisoned or disseised [have his rights or possessions taken away] or outlawed or exiled or in any way destroyed, nor will we go against him or send against him, except by the lawful judgment of his peers or by the law of the land." This basically meant that the government could punish citizens only by fairly and properly following the law.

Magna Carta continues to influence American law through the Bill of Rights. The most important example of Magna Carta's influence is the Fifth Amendment. Chapter 39 of Magna Carta is a direct forerunner of the clause, "No person shall be . . . deprived of life, liberty, or property, without due process of law." By the time the Fifth Amendment was written, "due process of law" had come to mean the same as "law of the land." In other words, the Fifth

Amendment says that the government cannot punish someone without fairly and properly following the law. (Unlike Magna Carta's chapter 39, however, the Fifth Amendment protects any "person," not just citizens.)

THE OTHER CHARTERS OF ENGLISH RIGHTS

The framers of the U.S. Constitution also claimed the rights declared in the Petition of Right of 1628 and the English Bill of Rights of 1689. The petition, which the English Parliament sent to Charles I (king of England from 1625 to 1649), is a statement of complaints against the king and of rights against the Crown (the royal branch of government). In the petition, Parliament declared that the king had violated the rights of his subjects (people under the monarch's rule) by taxing them without the consent of Parliament, putting them in prison without showing a good legal reason, forcing them to house soldiers, and using military law in times of peace.

The English Bill of Rights declares the rights of Parliament against the Crown. In 1689, King James II fled England after being removed from power. Prince William and Princess Mary of Orange (William's territory in southern France) accepted the throne. William was James's nephew and son-in-law, and Mary was James's daughter and William's wife. In return for the throne, William and Mary (now William III and Mary II) agreed to accept the Declaration of Rights, which Parliament later turned into the English Bill of Rights. The bill declared that certain acts of James II were then and from now on illegal.

The English Bill of Rights did not pretend to present any new principles. Nevertheless, the bargain between William and Mary and the English Parliament made Parliament supreme over the Crown. In this respect, the English Bill of Rights is unlike the American Bill of Rights, which limits the power of all branches of the national government—including the U.S. Congress. The English Bill of Rights declares certain rights also found in the American Bill of Rights, including the rights guaranteed by the Eighth Amendment. In fact, the Eighth Amendment is taken nearly word for word from the English Bill of Rights.

"Magna Charta is such a fellow, that he will have no sovereign [supreme ruler]."

—*Sir Edward Coke, speaker of the English Parliament's House of Commons, opposing a proposed change to the Petition of Right that would have upheld the supreme power of King Charles I over Parliament and the common law, May 17, 1628*

SIR EDWARD COKE
(1552–1634)

To support their claims to common law rights, the American colonists relied on the writings of English legal thinkers, especially the writings of Sir Edward Coke, who wrote several works on the common law. Coke's ideas on the common law greatly influenced English and American constitutional law.

Coke believed that the common law was above the monarch and Parliament; thus, neither the monarch nor Parliament could violate or take away common law rights, such as the right to trial by jury and the right to a speedy trial. In other words, Coke considered the common law to be supreme in the same way that the U.S. Constitution is (as it states in Article 6) the "supreme Law of the Land" in the United States.

During his life, Coke held many important positions in government, including attorney general (the Crown's lawyer), chief justice of the King's Bench (a trial court that hears major cases; this court is referred to as the Queen's Bench during the reign of a queen), and speaker of the English Parliament's House of Commons. As speaker of the House, Coke was a leading opponent of the English kings James I and Charles I. They believed that monarchs were above the common law and Parliament. In 1622, angered by Coke's criticisms of the Crown, King James I imprisoned Coke for nine months in the Tower of London, a prison for political criminals. In 1628, Coke helped to write the Petition of Right.

Coke's most important work was the four-volume *Institutes of the Laws of England,* published in 1641 after his death. The *Institutes* became a basic text for the study of law in England and America. The *Institutes* remained the standard legal text in America until well into the 18th century. Despite the influence of his conclusions, however, Coke's interpretations of early documents, such as Magna Carta, were often wrong.

Sir Edward Coke *(Library of Congress, Prints and Photographs Division [LC-USZ62-121998])*

John Winthrop (1588–1649) was the first governor of the Massachusetts Bay Colony, which adopted the Massachusetts Body of Liberties. *(Library of Congress, Prints and Photographs Division [LC-USZ62-124240])*

"Our ancestors were entitled to the common law of England when they emigrated [left England], that is, to just so much of it as they pleased to adopt, and no more. They were not bound or obliged to submit to it, unless they chose it."

—*American political leader John Adams, writing under the pen name "Novanglus" in 1774*

COLONIAL AMERICA

Although the first English settlers in America claimed the common law as their birthright, at least many had been unhappy with how justice was carried out in England. First, some settlers believed that the English system was out-of-date. For instance, English common law regarding crime was a confusing mix of precedents (earlier decisions that should be followed by judges deciding similar cases) and statutes written in law Latin and French. Therefore, in England, only the few who were educated could understand the common law of crime. The colonists simplified the law, published it in English, and made the law available for the general public. The colonists also often required that the law be read before certain public gatherings.

Also, the English often applied the law cruelly, unfairly, and unequally. For example, in England, death was the legal punishment for even the most minor crimes. But, England also did not punish all criminals the same for the same crime: For example, English courts allowed murderers who could read to escape death but sentenced thieves who could not read to hanging. Although the colonists did not ban the death penalty, they also allowed lesser punishments. For example, some colonies ended the death penalty for crimes of theft.

Colonists also stressed the rights of the accused in colonial laws. The accused is someone who has been arrested for or formally accused of a crime. The accused is also called the defendant. The rights of the accused included, among other rights, the right not to be tried (put on trial) twice for the same crime, the right not to be forced to confess, the right to a public trial, the right to trial by jury, the right to call and question witnesses, the right to be defended by a lawyer, and the right against cruel punishments. (Not every colony protected all of these rights.) These and other rights that limit the power of government to punish and to use force are now guaranteed by the Fourth through Eighth Amendments of the Bill of Rights. During the 18th century, however, the colonies began to focus more on maintaining order and less on expanding the rights of the accused.

THE MASSACHUSETTS BODY OF LIBERTIES
(1641)

To protect the religious purity of the new colony, the settlers of Massachusetts Bay first set up an oligarchy (government by the few) of magistrates. Soon, however, the colonists began to call for a popular government (government by the people). By 1634, the colony had replaced its oligarchy with a representative government (government by individuals chosen by the people). The colonists also demanded that the colony write a body of laws—similar to Magna Carta—describing the colonists' rights. Publishing such a body of laws would, the colonists believed, limit the magistrates' power.

In 1641, the Massachusetts legislature approved the Massachusetts Body of Liberties. A mix of Magna Carta, Puritan beliefs, and common law, the Body of Liberties was the first detailed American charter of fundamental rights. The law was far-reaching for its time. For example, besides guaranteeing the rights of male citizens, the Body of Liberties also guaranteed the rights of women, children, servants, foreigners living in the colony, and animals. The act also outlawed slavery. The Body of Liberties, however, failed to limit the magistrates' power. As a result, many of the colonists became unhappy with the law. In 1648, the colony replaced the Body of Liberties with the Massachusetts General Laws and Liberties. Nevertheless, the Body of Liberties became a model for other colonial laws, including the New York Charter of Liberties of 1683 and the Pennsylvania Charter of Privileges of 1701.

The Body of Liberties guaranteed many of the rights now found in the Bill of Rights. Moreover, the Body of Liberties was the first American document to guarantee some of these rights, including some of the rights guaranteed by the Fourth through Eighth Amendments. These rights include the right not to be tried twice for the same crime, the right to be paid for private property taken by the government for public use, the right to a lawyer, the right to trial by jury, and the right against cruel punishments. Most of the rights guaranteed by the Body of Liberties, however, were more limited than such rights are today. For example, it allowed torture in certain cases involving capital crimes. The Body of Liberties is an important forerunner of the Bill of Rights in another way: The Body of Liberties was not the grant of a ruler, but the first American charter of fundamental rights that the people's representatives made into law.

The Puritan colonies of New England followed English criminal law less closely than did other colonies. (New England consists of what are now the six northeastern U.S. states of Maine, New

Hampshire, Vermont, Massachusetts, Rhode Island, and Connecticut.) The Puritans believed in strictly following the Bible. Like other American colonies, the Puritan colonies drew most of their law from English law. Some Puritan colonies, such as Massachusetts and Connecticut, however, drew much of their law from the Bible. For example, in English law, serious property crimes were usually capital crimes (crimes punishable by death). On the other hand, Massachusetts and Connecticut punished property crimes less harshly, but made crimes such as adultery (being unfaithful to one's wife or husband) capital crimes. In England, adultery was a much less serious crime. Although laws in these colonies were harsh, magistrates (local judges) usually reduced the punishment if criminals gave some sign that they felt sorry for their crimes.

THE ROAD TO REVOLUTION

In the years after the French and Indian War, the British Parliament raised taxes or imposed new taxes on certain goods in the American colonies in order to raise money to help cover the costs of defending Britain's now bigger empire in North America. The British also imposed certain rules on shipped goods in order to stop the colonists from smuggling goods (illegally bringing in goods from, or sending them to, another country). The war, which lasted from 1754 to 1763, was the last of a series of four wars fought since 1689 in North America between Britain and France, with their Native American and colonial allies. Although Britain defeated France, the war left Britain with a heavy debt and the great costs of managing and defending the new North American territory that the country gained during the war.

The colonists protested that these taxes violated the colonists' English right against taxation without representation: They could be taxed, they claimed, only with their consent, or the consent of their representatives. No one represented the colonists in the British Parliament. Thus, the colonists argued, only their colonial legislatures could tax the colonies.

The colonists also reacted violently against the taxes. Colonists destroyed and refused to buy taxed goods, and threatened and attacked customs officers, who collected the taxes that Britain imposed on goods imported (brought into) the colonies. The more the colonists resisted, the more Parliament felt that it needed to show its power over the colonies and to show the right of the British government to tax them. Over time, the conflict between the American colonies and Britain grew into war. On April 19, 1775, colonists and British soldiers exchanged the opening shots of

During the reign of George III, king of Great Britain and Ireland from 1760 to 1820, the policies of the British government toward the American colonies led to the American Revolution. *(Library of Congress, Prints and Photographs Division [LC-USZ62-93478])*

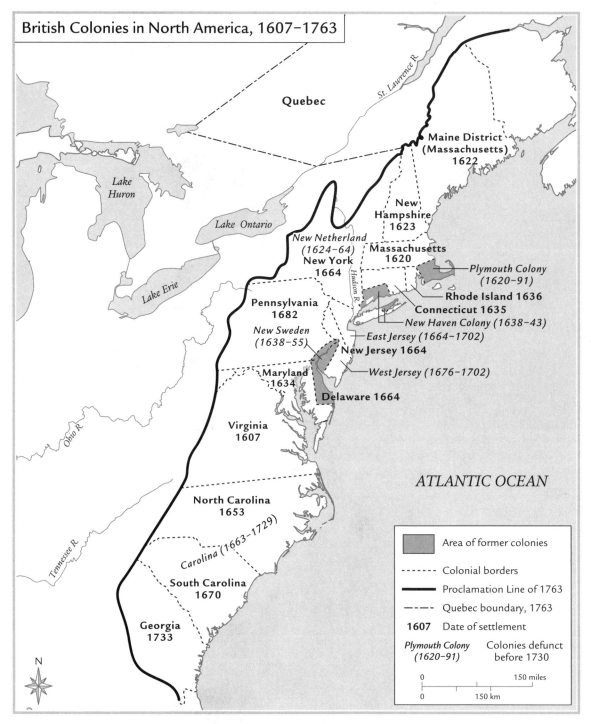

British Colonies in North America, 1607–1763

Quebec

St. Lawrence R.

Lake Huron

Lake Ontario

Lake Erie

Ohio R.

Tennessee R.

Maine District (Massachusetts) 1622

New Hampshire 1623

New Netherland (1624–64)
New York 1664

Massachusetts 1620

Hudson R.

Plymouth Colony (1620–91)

Rhode Island 1636
Connecticut 1635

Pennsylvania 1682

New Sweden (1638–55)

New Haven Colony (1638–43)

East Jersey (1664–1702)
New Jersey 1664

West Jersey (1676–1702)

Maryland 1634

Delaware 1664

Virginia 1607

ATLANTIC OCEAN

North Carolina 1653

Carolina (1663–1729)

South Carolina 1670

Georgia 1733

N

▨	Area of former colonies
------	Colonial borders
——	Proclamation Line of 1763
—·—	Quebec boundary, 1763
1607	Date of settlement
Plymouth Colony (1620–91)	Colonies defunct before 1730

0   150 miles
0   150 km

In the Proclamation of 1763, Great Britain declared that the area west of the Proclamation Line was Native American territory. In 1776, the American colonies declared independence from Great Britain because they believed that Britain had violated their traditional rights as English people.

This 18th-century print shows John Malcolm, a British customs officer, about to be tarred and feathered by Boston colonists. In the years leading to the American Revolution, colonists reacted against British taxes on imports by threatening and attacking British customs officers. *(Library of Congress, Prints and Photographs Division [LC-USZ62-45556])*

the American Revolution in the Massachusetts towns of Lexington and Concord.

REVOLUTIONARY AMERICA

By 1776, the American colonists lost all hope that they could settle their differences with Great Britain peacefully and remain part of the British Empire. The colonies began formally changing themselves into states. In May, the Continental Congress (the government of the United States during the American Revolution) called for the colonies to set up their own governments. On July 4, 1776, the Continental Congress declared in the Declaration of Independence that "these United Colonies are, and of Right ought to be

Free and Independent States." By the end of the American Revolution in 1783, all of the 13 states had adopted their own constitutions.

Experience had taught the former colonists that their state constitutions had to be more than just blueprints for setting up governments. When Americans were still colonists, their royal governors constantly challenged the right of the colonies to govern themselves through their legislatures. To defend that right, the colonists would appeal to fundamental law, such as Magna Carta.

Leaders of the Second Continental Congress. The Second Continental Congress, which first met on May 10, 1775, was the congress of the United States during the American Revolution. The Second Continental Congress was the forerunner of the U.S. Congress. *Left to right:* John Adams, delegate from Massachusetts; Gouverneur Morris, delegate from New York; Alexander Hamilton, delegate from New York; and Thomas Jefferson, delegate from Virginia. *(Library of Congress, Prints and Photographs Division [LC-USZ62-14414])*

THE VIRGINIA DECLARATION OF RIGHTS
(1776)

Virginia, the oldest and largest of the original American states, was the first state to adopt a declaration of rights and a constitution. The Virginia Declaration of Rights (adopted June 12, 1776) and the Virginia Constitution (adopted June 29, 1776) are also older than the Declaration of Independence. The author of the Virginia Declaration of Rights was George Mason, one of the delegates at the Constitutional Convention of 1787 who refused to sign the U.S. Constitution because it did not have a bill of rights. Mason also wrote much of the Virginia Constitution. James Madison, who helped to write the Virginia Constitution, used the Virginia Declaration of Rights as a model when (as representative of Virginia in the U.S. Congress) he wrote the amendments that became the Bill of Rights.

The Virginia Declaration of Rights guaranteed many of the rights now guaranteed in the Fourth through Eighth Amendments of the Bill of Rights, including (in the words of the declaration) the right to a "speedy trial," the right to trial by jury, the right not "to give evidence against" oneself, the right not to be "deprived of . . . liberty except by the law of the land," the right to confront "accusers and witnesses," and the right against "cruel and unusual punishments."

The colonists' arguments were less forceful, however, when they were based on unwritten principles. By the time they were ready to write their first state constitutions, Americans believed that constitutions had to guarantee certain individual rights and set specific limits to government power. Nine states introduced their state constitutions with bills of rights. The other four states (New Jersey, Georgia, New York, and South Carolina) added specific rights into the bodies of the state constitutions. Together, these first state constitutions guaranteed nearly all of the rights now guaranteed by the Fourth through Eighth Amendments (although not necessarily in the same way or to the same extent).

The Declaration of Independence was signed on July 4, 1776. *(Library of Congress, Prints and Photographs Division [LC-USZ62-3736])*

Sir William Blackstone (1723–80), English judge and legal scholar, wrote *Commentaries on the Laws of England,* 4 vol. (1765–69). This was the standard textbook for the teaching of law in England and North America. The *Commentaries* greatly influenced American lawmakers and legal thinkers during and after the American Revolution. *(Library of Congress, Prints and Photographs Division [LC-USZ62-43798])*

THE BIRTH OF THE BILL OF RIGHTS

The U.S. Constitution set up a federal system of government in the United States. Under a federal system, power is divided between a central government and the states. The central government is also called the federal government. When the writers of the U.S. Constitution presented it to the Constitutional Convention on September 12, 1787, George Mason, a delegate from Virginia, wished aloud that the Constitution "had been prefaced [introduced] with a Bill of Rights," which would limit the powers of the federal government. Elbridge Gerry (a delegate from Massachusetts) and Edmund Randolph (a delegate from Virginia) also wanted a bill of rights that would limit the powers of the federal government. The Constitutional Convention, however, rejected the idea. On September 17, the last day of the convention, Mason, Gerry, and Randolph refused to sign the Constitution.

Why so many of the convention's delegates rejected a federal bill of rights is unclear. Perhaps the delegates, who had already spent months working on the Constitution during the hottest summer in Philadelphia that anyone could remember, were ready to go home. The delegates were probably not eager to deal with such a big issue when their job was almost done. Perhaps the delegates also agreed with Roger Sherman, a delegate from Connecticut. He argued that a federal bill of rights was not needed: The state bills of rights, he claimed, were enough to protect the rights of Americans. Also, he argued, the federal government had only those powers named in the Constitution, which did not give the federal government any power to violate rights protected by the states.

Although the Constitution as adopted in 1787 did not contain a bill of rights, it did protect some rights normally protected by a bill of rights. For example, under Article 1, Section 9 of the Constitution, the government cannot punish people without a trial or punish them for doing something that was not a crime at the time. Article 3, Section 2 guarantees the right to trial by jury in criminal cases.

"A bill of rights is what the people are entitled to against every government on earth, general or particular, and what no just government should refuse."

—Thomas Jefferson, in a letter dated December 20, 1787, sent from Paris, France, to James Madison, a leading Federalist

"I am glad to hear that the new constitution is received with favor. I sincerely wish that the 9 first conventions may receive, and the 4 last reject it. The former will secure it finally, while the latter will oblige them to offer a declaration of rights in order to complete the union."

—Thomas Jefferson, in a letter dated February 6, 1788, sent from Paris, France, to Federalist James Madison

The Constitution of the United States was signed at the Constitutional Convention in Philadelphia, Pennsylvania, on September 17, 1787. *(Library of Congress, Prints and Photographs Division [LC-USA7-34630])*

James Madison (1751–1836) was the most important framer of the U.S. Constitution and author of the amendments that were later shaped into the Bill of Rights. Madison became the fourth president of the United States in 1809. *(Library of Congress, Prints and Photographs Division [LC-USZ62-106865])*

"For why declare that things shall not be done which [the government has] no power to do?"

—*Federalist Alexander Hamilton, on why the U.S. Constitution did not need a bill of rights, in* The Federalist, *no. 84, 1788*

The Constitutional Convention's decision not to include a bill of rights in the Constitution turned out to be a serious mistake. The lack of a bill of rights was the most powerful argument of the Anti-Federalists (those who opposed the Constitution). The Anti-Federalists believed that the federal government under the proposed Constitution would be too powerful. Mason and Gerry were leading Anti-Federalists. The Federalists (those who supported the Constitution) countered, as Sherman had argued, that a federal bill of rights was unnecessary: The Congress, the Federalists claimed, would have no power to violate individual liberties.

In the end, the Federalists' arguments against a federal bill of rights were unconvincing. By January 9, 1788, five states (Delaware, Pennsylvania, New Jersey, Georgia, and Connecticut) had ratified (formally approved) the Constitution. Only four more states had to ratify the Constitution for it to become the law of the land. What important states such as Massachusetts, New York, and Virginia would decide, however, remained uncertain. To win the support of Massachusetts, the sixth state to ratify the Constitution, Federalist delegates to that state's convention proposed a list of amendments (changes in wording or meaning) to the Constitution. Massachusetts was the first among the states that ratified the Constitution to submit proposed amendments along with the state's ratification to Congress. Other states that ratified the Constitution also officially recommended amendments. New Hampshire, the ninth state to ratify the Constitution, ratified the Constitution on June 21, 1788.

When the first American congress under the new U.S. Constitution met in April 1789, James Madison, representative from Virginia and a leading Federalist, led the effort to amend the Constitution. Madison drew the amendments that became the Bill of Rights from those proposed by the states, especially the amendments proposed by Virginia. The United States adopted the Bill of Rights on December 15, 1791.

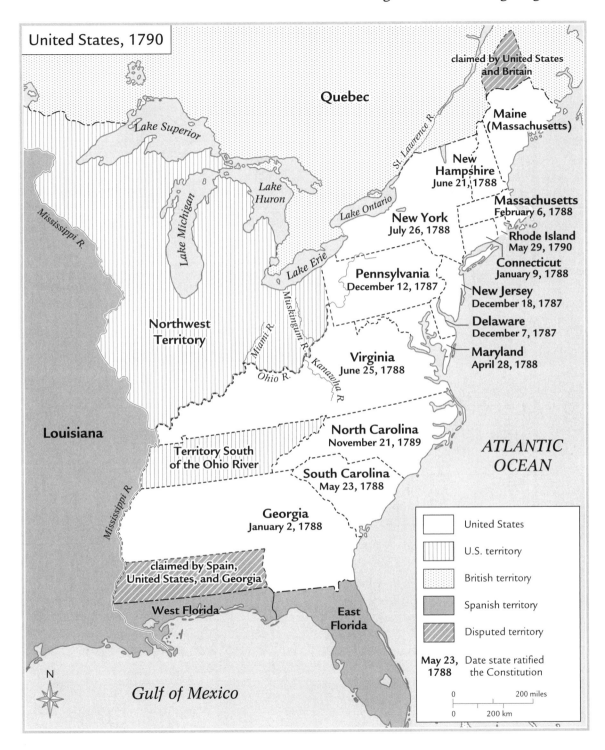

United States, 1790

claimed by United States and Britain

Quebec

Maine (Massachusetts)

Lake Superior

St. Lawrence R.

New Hampshire
June 21, 1788

Lake Michigan   *Lake Huron*

Lake Ontario

New York
July 26, 1788

Massachusetts
February 6, 1788

Rhode Island
May 29, 1790

Lake Erie

Connecticut
January 9, 1788

Mississippi R.

Pennsylvania
December 12, 1787

New Jersey
December 18, 1787

Muskingum R.

Northwest Territory

Miami R.

Ohio R.   *Kanawha R.*

Delaware
December 7, 1787

Maryland
April 28, 1788

Virginia
June 25, 1788

Louisiana

North Carolina
November 21, 1789

Territory South of the Ohio River

Mississippi R.

South Carolina
May 23, 1788

ATLANTIC OCEAN

Georgia
January 2, 1788

claimed by Spain, United States, and Georgia

West Florida

East Florida

	United States
	U.S. territory
	British territory
	Spanish territory
	Disputed territory

May 23, 1788   Date state ratified the Constitution

N

Gulf of Mexico

0   200 miles
0   200 km

FROM STATES' RIGHTS TO THE RIGHTS OF INDIVIDUALS

When the United States adopted the Bill of Rights, it guaranteed rights against the federal government, not the states. In 1868, however, the United States adopted the Fourteenth Amendment, which forbids the states (as the Fifth Amendment forbids the federal government) from depriving "any person of life, liberty, or property, without due process of law." In other words, the Fourteenth Amendment says that state governments (just like the federal government) cannot treat people unfairly under the law. (After the American Civil War, the Thirteenth, Fourteenth, and Fifteenth Amendments made the newly freed black slaves full American citizens.)

The Fourteenth Amendment changed the Bill of Rights from a document that stressed the rights of the states to one that also forbids state and local governments from violating the fundamental rights of individuals. In the 20th century, the U.S. Supreme Court said in a number of decisions that the due process clause of the Fourteenth Amendment forbids the states from violating rights guaranteed in the Bill of Rights. For example, in *Gitlow v. New York* (1925), the Court said that the due process clause forbids the states from violating the First Amendment right to free speech. In *Wolf v. Colorado* (1949), the Court said that the due process clause forbids the states from violating the Fourth Amendment right against unreasonable searches and seizures. Today, all but the Second and Seventh Amendments, and one clause in the Fifth Amendment, apply to state and local governments. The Fifth Amendment clause that does not apply to the states is the one that forbids the federal government from trying someone for a crime unless a grand jury agrees that the government has enough evidence against the accused.

The Right Against Unreasonable Searches and Seizures

2

The right of the people to be secure in their persons, houses, papers, and effects, against unreasonable searches and seizures, shall not be violated, and no Warrants shall issue, but upon probable cause, supported by Oath or affirmation, and particularly describing the place to be searched, and the persons or things to be seized.

—Amendment IV, Constitution of the United States

Under the Fourth Amendment, Americans have a "right . . . against unreasonable searches and seizures." This means that an officer (for example, a sheriff or a police officer) cannot search or arrest (take or hold) people, or search or take away their things (such as their homes or papers), without a good legal reason.

The amendment also says that no warrants can be issued without "probable cause." A *warrant* is a writ (a written legal order) that gives an officer the power to do something that is necessary in order to carry out the law. In the Fourth Amendment, the word "Warrants" refers specifically to search and arrest warrants. A search warrant gives an officer the power to search a place or a person. A search warrant also usually gives an officer the power to seize (take or take control of) evidence (something that is presented in court in order to prove whether something is true or false). An arrest warrant orders an officer to arrest the person named on the warrant and to bring him or her before the court or a magistrate (a court officer who has some of the powers of judges, such as the power to issue warrants).

An officer cannot receive a warrant unless he or she can show "probable cause," that is, good reason (reason based on facts) for believing that (1) something illegal has been or is being done, (2) the person to be arrested is guilty of breaking the law, (3) the thing to be seized is in the place named on the warrant, or (4) a search will uncover illegal goods.

Finally, the Fourth Amendment requires that warrants be specific. They must "particularly [describe] the place to be searched, and the persons or things to be seized."

ORIGINS

Americans created the Fourth Amendment because they disliked writs of assistance when America was under British rule. Generally, a writ of assistance is a writ issued to a sheriff, marshal, or other law officer to enforce an order. In the American colonies, Great Britain used writs of assistance to search for illegally imported goods. (Importing certain goods into the colonies without paying British taxes was illegal.) These writs allowed British customs officers to search anyone and anywhere and to seize any smuggled goods the offficers may find. Also, these writs remained in force until six months after the death of the monarch.

These writs of assistance were general warrants, writs stating that those legally bearing the warrants had been given power by the monarch to arrest, search, or seize whomever or whatever in order to carry out the law. Besides using such warrants to find smuggled goods, British officers used general warrants to search for and arrest political and religious dissenters. Americans created the Fourth Amendment mainly in order to outlaw general warrants in America.

Although the American colonists disliked Britain's use or (as they would say) abuse of general warrants, the American colonies also used them, including writs of assistance. Most colonies used general searches to collect taxes, discourage illegal hunting or fishing, capture serious criminals, or find stolen goods. Although specific warrants (that is, warrants that limit searches, seizures, and arrests to the particular person, things, or place named on the warrant) did exist, the colonies rarely used them before 1750. General warrants were still common in America during the American Revolution, even though eight state constitutions outlawed general warrants.

During the 17th and 18th centuries, respected English legal thinkers, such as Coke, Sir Matthew Hale, and Sir William Black-

"There are . . . essential rights, which we have justly understood to be the rights of freemen; as freedom from hasty and unreasonable search warrants, warrants not founded on oath, and not issued with due caution, for searching and seizing men's papers, property, and persons."

—Anti-Federalist Richard Henry Lee, on the need for constitutional protection against unreasonable search warrants, The Federal Farmer, *no. 4, October 12, 1787*

stone, argued that general warrants violated Magna Carta, specifically chapter 39, which says, "No freemen shall be captured or imprisoned or disseised or outlawed or exiled or in any way destroyed, nor will we go against him or send against him, except by the lawful judgment of his peers or by the law of the land." In fact, however, Magna Carta says nothing against general searches. Nevertheless, Magna Carta became an important weapon against them.

As *Paxton's Case* (1761) shows, resistance to general warrants also existed in America. In 1760, the death of Britain's king George II meant that existing writs of assistance would end after six months. In *Paxton's Case*, 63 Boston merchants asked the Massachusetts Superior Court (the highest court in the colony) not to replace the writs. Representing the merchants, James Otis, Jr., a Massachusetts lawyer, argued before the court that the 1662 British statute approving writs of assistance violated common law. He also argued that the statute violated natural law. Those who believed in this system of law or justice believed that it comes from nature and that natural law can be discovered by human reason alone, without

"EVERY MAN'S HOUSE IS HIS CASTLE"

Critics of general warrants often referred to *Semayne's Case* (1603), which upheld the right of homeowners to defend their homes against those who are entering illegally, even if the invaders are acting on behalf of the monarch. Said the court, "The house of every one is to him as his castle and fortress." This restated the popular English saying, "A man's house is his castle," which has been traced back to 1567. Forty years after *Semayne's Case*, Coke said in his *Institutes of the Laws of England* "For a man's house is his castle."

Semayne's Case, however, did recognize the right of officers to break into someone's home, after giving notice, to make an arrest or to present an order to appear in court. But although *Semayne's Case* upheld the right of the government to invade a dwelling in order to carry out a legal order, the saying "Every man's house is his castle" became a popular rallying cry against general searches.

referring to human laws and decisions by judges. People who believed in natural law also believed that it is common to all human societies and that it is the proper basis for all human laws. "A man's house is his castle," said Otis, repeating the popular English saying. He continued, "This writ [of assistance], if it should be declared legal, would totally [destroy] this privilege."

To support his argument that writs of assistance violated common law, Otis referred to Coke, who had argued that Magna Carta forbids general search warrants. (In fact, as already noted, Magna Carta says nothing against general searches.) Otis also wrongly interpreted Coke to mean that all search warrants must be specific. In the end, the court rejected Otis's arguments and decided in favor of continuing to issue writs of assistance.

The Massachusetts legislature responded to the court's decision by reducing the judges' salaries and passing a bill to define writs of assistance as specific warrants. The state governor, however, vetoed the bill. Chief Justice Thomas Hutchinson would later argue that his support of writs of assistance in *Paxton's Case* had led to his political downfall. Also, less than a decade later, most colonial courts would refuse to issue writs of assistance when called for by the Townshend Acts of 1767. (The acts taxed certain goods imported into the American colonies.)

Although opposition to general warrants has its roots in Great Britain, the history of specific warrants begins in 18th-century Massachusetts. Specific warrants name the particular place that is to be searched and the person or things that are to be searched, arrested, or seized. Moreover, specific warrants limit all searches, arrests, and seizures to the particular place, person, or things listed on the warrant. From 1756 to 1766, a group of Massachusetts statutes and court decisions limited a search or an arrest to the person or place named on the warrant. In the 1780s, the state legislature also limited seizures of objects to those things named on the warrant.

JAMES OTIS, JR.
(1725–1783)

American colonial political leader and lawyer James Otis, Jr., was born in West Barnstable, Massachusetts, in 1725. Otis, famous largely for *Paxton's Case* (1761), greatly influenced the ideas of the American Revolution. Although Otis lost *Paxton's Case*, he soon became leader of the radical wing of colonists who opposed Great Britain's policies regarding the American colonies. Otis also defended colonial rights in speeches and pamphlets. *Paxton's Case* led to Otis's being elected in May 1761 to the Massachusetts House of Representatives, to which he was reelected almost every year until his political life ended in 1769. Although Otis was elected speaker of the house in 1766, the royal governor of Massachusetts vetoed his election.

In 1769, Otis was struck on the head during a quarrel with a British customs officer. The blow made Otis, who had already tended to have fits of insanity, permanently (but harmlessly) insane. He died in 1783 after being struck by lightning.

James Otis, Jr. *(Library of Congress, Prints and Photographs Division [LC-USZ62-102561])*

UNREASONABLE SEARCHES AND SEIZURES

The Fourth Amendment does not say what is an "unreasonable" search or seizure. Nor does the amendment clearly say whether a search or seizure not approved by a warrant is necessarily unreasonable. In cases before *Harris v. United States* (1947), the U.S. Supreme Court tended to define a reasonable search or seizure as one that, with narrow exceptions, is approved by a proper warrant. Starting with *Harris* and until *Chimel v. California* (1969), however, the Court did not presume that searches and seizures require warrants to be reasonable, although the Court believed that whether a search or seizure was approved by a warrant is one among other issues that should be considered. Since *Chimel,* the Court has, as it did before *Harris,* stressed the importance of warrants.

In many cases, before and after *Harris,* the Court stressed that only a neutral magistrate should issue search and arrest warrants. That is, unlike the officer requesting the warrant, the magistrate must have no interest in whether the search or arrest takes place. After the officer applying for the warrant swears that the information given on the application is true, the magistrate must determine whether there is probable cause for a search or an arrest.

Even though the Court has often stressed the importance of warrants, the Court has never believed that the Fourth Amendment requires officers to get warrants for all searches and seizures. First of all, getting a warrant may be impractical. For instance, while arresting someone, police officers often search that person for any hidden weapons or evidence. A search connected with a proper arrest is called a "search incident to arrest." In *Weeks v. United States* (1914), the Court recognized the power of officers to do such searches without a warrant. No justice has ever challenged the principle, which is rooted in common law, that officers making a proper arrest can search the person being arrested for hidden weapons or evidence. In *Chimel,* the Court limited the search of someone in a search incident to arrest to the area "within his immediate control," meaning, the area from where the person may get a weapon or evidence that can be destroyed. The great majority of searches are searches incident to arrest.

Other searches that do not require warrants are stop-and-frisk searches. When police officers see someone acting suspiciously but do not have probable cause to arrest that person, they often stop the suspect and frisk (run their hands quickly over) the suspect's clothing to find any hidden weapons. In *Terry v. Ohio* (1968), the Court said that before an officer can stop and frisk someone, the officer must have reasons, based on facts, to believe that the suspect is about to commit a crime and that the officer's safety or the safety of others is at risk.

Today, many searches do not require warrants. Warrants are now most often required in criminal cases. However, there are

A police officer frisks seven men in New York City as they line up on a fence. *(Library of Congress, Prints and Photographs Division [LC-USZ62-120785])*

exceptions here as well. For example, officials can search public schools, government offices, and prisons without warrants. Other searches that do not require warrants include automobile searches; body searches (including those that involve extracting blood); ship searches; border searches (searches of people, vehicles, or goods entering the country); "open field" searches (searches in open areas, like pastures, wooded areas, open water, and vacant lots); and plain view searches (searches of illegal items that are not blocked from an officer's view).

THE EXCLUSIONARY RULE

The Fourth Amendment does not say whether evidence obtained by violating the amendment should be barred from being used against the accused. Before the 20th century, the U.S. Supreme Court followed common law, which allowed the government to use illegally seized evidence against defendants in criminal trials. The Court said that victims of illegal searches or seizures could seek justice by suing the officers who had violated the law.

In *Weeks,* the Court decided that the Fourth Amendment does bar the government from using evidence obtained from an illegal search or seizure by federal officers. This decision established the exclusionary rule, which bars evidence obtained by violating the constitutional rights of defendants. The Court said, however, that the exclusionary rule applies only to federal, not state, criminal cases. In *Wolf v. Colorado* (1949), the Court said that the states cannot violate the Fourth Amendment right against unreasonable searches and seizures. But the Court still refused to require the states to follow the exclusionary rule. In *Mapp v. Ohio* (1961), however, the Court reversed itself and said that the exclusionary rule also applies to the states.

Mapp involved the case of Dollree Mapp. In 1957, in Cleveland, Ohio, three police officers entered the boardinghouse of Mapp without a search warrant. The officers believed that Mapp was hiding someone involved in a recent bombing. They also expected to find evidence of illegal gambling. When they entered the boardinghouse, they found neither the person they were looking for nor evidence of illegal gambling. They did find, however, illegal pornography (sexual pictures or writings), for which Mapp was arrested and convicted (found guilty) for possessing. Overturning Mapp's conviction, the Court said that evidence seized by violating the Fourth Amendment cannot be used against criminal defendants in state courts, just as such evidence cannot be used against criminal defendants in federal courts.

Many criticized the Court's decision in *Mapp.* Supporters of the exclusionary rule claimed that it is the only way to protect the right to be free from illegal searches or seizures. Critics, however, argued that a criminal should not escape punishment because a police officer violated the U.S. Constitution. Critics also argued that the exclusionary rule does not strongly discourage police officers from violating the Fourth Amendment. For example, the rule does not require superiors to punish police officers who obtained evidence illegally. Moreover, governments rarely try to bring such officers to trial.

Since the 1960s, the Court has limited the exclusionary rule in important ways. For instance, in most cases, only victims of illegal searches can benefit from the exclusionary rule. For example, according to the Court's decision in *Rakas v. Illinois* (1978), if officers violate the Fourth Amendment by searching Mary's house and find evidence against Jane, the evidence can be used against Jane in her trial. State courts, however, are free to exclude evidence in cases like Jane's. Also, in *Harris v. New York* (1971), the Court allowed prosecutors to use illegally obtained evidence to challenge a defendant's testimony (statements made under oath by a witness) in court. In *United States v. Calandra* (1974), the Court allowed prosecutors to admit illegally obtained evidence in grand jury proceedings. In *Chapman v. California* (1967), the Court allowed higher courts to consider whether the use of illegally obtained evidence in a criminal trial was harmless error, an error that neither affected an important or essential right nor changed the outcome of a trial.

Byron R. White, associate justice of the U.S. Supreme Court from 1962 to 1993, delivered the decision in *United States v. Leon* (1984), which allowed good faith exceptions to the exclusionary rule. *(Library of Congress, Prints and Photographs Division [LC-USZ62-60144])*

In *United States v. Leon* (1984), the Court allowed "good faith" exceptions to the exclusionary rule. In cases where a search warrant is found later by a higher court to be illegal, the good faith exception allows the government to use the evidence that was obtained under the warrant against the defendant in a trial if the police reasonably believed at the time that the warrant was legal. The good faith exception has become the most important exception to the exclusionary rule.

The exclusionary rule also applies to evidence obtained by violating the Fifth and Sixth Amendments. For example, the government cannot use coerced confessions from defendants as evidence against them in criminal trials, since forcing defendants to confess violates their Fifth Amendment right not to accuse themselves of a crime. The government also cannot use statements from defendants as evidence against them in criminal trials if officers obtain the statements by violating the defendants' Sixth Amendment right to a lawyer.

EXPECTATION OF PRIVACY

Before 1967, the U.S. Supreme Court believed that the Fourth Amendment was meant to protect property interests. This view controlled the Court's decisions in many cases, including a case involving wiretapping. Wiretapping involves connecting into a telephone or telegraph wire to get information by secretly listening to private conversations. In *Olmstead v. United States* (1928), the Court said that wiretapping is not a search or a seizure within the meaning of the Fourth Amendment. Therefore, the Court said, the government did not need a warrant in order to wiretap someone's telephone conversations, as long as the government did not physically enter the person's property without permission or by force.

Warrantless wiretapping continued to be legal for almost 40 years until the Court's decision in *Katz v. United States* (1967). In *Katz,* the Court said that the main purpose of the Fourth Amendment is to protect privacy, not property. Thus, overruling its decision in *Olmstead,* the Court said that the Fourth Amendment requires the government to get a search warrant to install a wiretap.

Katz involved the case of Charles Katz. Agents from the Federal Bureau of Investigation (FBI) suspected that Katz was illegally sending gambling information over the telephone from Los Angeles, California, to clients in other states. Without a warrant, the agents attached an electronic listening and recording device to the roof of a public telephone booth where Katz made his calls. Based on recordings of Katz's telephone conversations, Katz was convicted of illegally sending betting information from Los Angeles to Boston, Massachusetts, and Miami, Florida.

The Court said that the government, by "electronically listening to and recording" Katz's conversations, violated Katz's privacy, "upon which he justifiably relied while using the telephone booth"; therefore, the wiretapping was a search and seizure within the meaning of the Fourth Amendment. The Fourth Amendment, therefore, required the agents to get a search warrant to wiretap the public pay phone, even though the agents did not physically enter the phone booth. In a separate opinion, Justice John Marshall Harlan said "that an enclosed telephone booth is an area where, like a home, . . . and unlike a field, . . . a person has a constitutionally protected reasonable expectation of privacy."

"The Fourth Amendment protects people, not places. What a person knowingly exposes to the public, even in his own home or office, is not a subject of Fourth Amendment protection. . . . But what he seeks to preserve as private, even in an area accessible to the public, may be constitutionally protected."

—*Associate Justice Potter Stewart, delivering the opinion of the U.S. Supreme Court in* Katz v. United States *(1967)*

Since *Katz,* whether a search or seizure violates a "reasonable expectation of privacy" has determined whether a search or seizure is presumed to require a warrant. Now, however, the Court tries to determine whether the expectation of privacy is so great that a search or seizure requires a warrant. In *Cardwell v. Lewis* (1974), Associate Justice Harry A. Blackmun, who delivered the opinion of the Court, said, "One has a lesser expectation of privacy in a motor vehicle" than in a home or an office. If there is a lesser expectation of privacy, then a search or seizure may not require a warrant. As a result, the power of the government to search greatly expanded after *Katz.*

NATIONAL SECURITY

U.S. courts have generally accepted the power of the president to approve warrantless searches and seizures (such as break-ins and spying) in order to gather foreign intelligence (information about possible or actual foreign enemies of the United States or about other countries). There are good reasons for allowing presidents this power: For instance, to counter foreign threats, presidents have to act secretly and quickly. Also, presidents know much more about foreign affairs and have more experience in such matters than do judges. Finally, the U.S. Constitution gives presidents the dominant role in foreign affairs.

Since Franklin D. Roosevelt (U.S. president from 1933 to 1945), American presidents have also claimed the power to approve warrantless searches and seizures, including warrantless electronic surveillance, to protect national security. *Electronic surveillance* means spying through the use of electronic devices, such as wiretaps, bugs (hidden listening devices), and videotape recorders. In *United States v. United States District Court* (1972), however, the Court said that, even in matters of national security, the federal government must get a warrant to spy within the United States in order to gather domestic intelligence (information about groups or individuals within the country). Limits on gathering domestic intelligence is meant to prevent the creation

Lewis F. Powell, Jr., associate justice of the U.S. Supreme Court from 1972 to 1987, delivered the decision in *United States v. United States District Court* (1972), which required the federal government to get a warrant in order to spy within the United States. Congress has since given the federal government more power to spy on Americans. *(Library of Congress, Prints and Photographs Division [LC-USZ62-60140])*

of a secret police, a police organization that works mostly in secrecy. In many countries, the secret police suppresses dissent, often by inspiring fear.

In 1976, the Senate Select Committee to Study Governmental Operations with Respect to Intelligence Activities issued a final report providing evidence of many cases where, from the 1930s to the 1970s, the executive branch and intelligence agencies illegally or improperly used their power to spy electronically. (The executive branch includes the president, the vice president, and the president's advisers.) For example, from 1940 to 1975, the FBI installed about 10,000 wiretaps and bugs. Other federal agencies also wiretapped phones and planted bugs. An agent in the Department of the Treasury installed more than 10,000 wiretaps and microphones between 1934 and 1948.

Although these agencies conducted such spying in the name of national security, in most cases, they spied in order to control crime or to keep an eye on political dissenters. For example, between 1963 and 1968, the FBI spied on civil rights activist Martin Luther King, Jr., in search of "communist" influence. (During the 1950s and 1960s, King was an important leader in the movement to gain equal rights for African Americans.) During the 1960s and the 1970s, the Central Intelligence Agency (which gathers foreign intelligence) illegally spied on thousands of activists within the United States and abroad in order to find ties between antiwar groups and foreign powers. The agency never found any such ties.

The many cases of improper and illegal electronic spying by the federal government led Congress to pass the Foreign Intelligence Surveillance Act (FISA) in 1978. The act required that spying within the United States against a foreign power or an agent of a foreign power in order to protect national security be approved by a warrant. Foreign powers include, for example, foreign governments, foreign political groups, and international terrorist groups. An agent of a

Under J. Edgar Hoover, director of the Federal Bureau of Investigation from 1924 to 1972, the FBI spied on many Americans in an effort to find communist influence. *(Library of Congress, Prints and Photographs Division [LC-USZ62-92411])*

foreign power is someone who works for or on behalf of a foreign power. FISA established a special secret court, which reviews applications by the federal government to spy against foreign powers or agents of foreign powers. The act also banned the government from using electronic devices to listen in on Americans unless their activities involve criminal conduct.

Twenty years later, however, the terrorist attacks on September 11, 2001, against the United States would lead Congress to expand the power of the federal government in order to deal with the threat of global terrorism (the use of violence to frighten people into accepting certain political goals or demands). Weeks after the terrorist attacks, Congress passed the USA PATRIOT Act, which gave the federal government much more power to search and spy in order to gather foreign and domestic intelligence. For example, the act changed FISA to allow the FBI to do searches and to wiretap in criminal investigations without having to show probable cause if gathering foreign intelligence is an important reason (rather than *the* reason) for the search or wiretap.

On August 9, 1974, U.S. president Richard M. Nixon resigned from office because of the Watergate affair, a series of scandals involving, among other things, illegal wiretapping of citizens by members of the executive branch while he was president and political spying by his reelection committee. He had been president since 1969. *(Library of Congress, Prints and Photographs Division [LC-USZ62-13037])*

3

The Right to
Fair Treatment

No person shall be held to answer for a capital, or otherwise infamous crime, unless on a presentment or indictment of a Grand Jury, except in cases arising in the land or naval forces, or in the Militia, when in actual service in time of War or public danger; nor shall any person be subject for the same offence to be twice put in jeopardy of life or limb; nor shall be compelled in any criminal case to be a witness against himself, nor be deprived of life, liberty, or property, without due process of law; nor shall private property be taken for public use, without just compensation.

—Amendment V, Constitution of the United States

The rights guaranteed by the Fifth Amendment help to ensure that the government treats people fairly under the law. The right to an indictment by a grand jury, the right against double jeopardy, and the right against self-incrimination are meant to protect people against unfair and unjustified prosecutions. The right to due process of law forbids the government from depriving people "of life, liberty, or property" unfairly. Finally, the right to just compensation requires the government to pay a fair price for private property taken for public use.

THE RIGHT TO
INDICTMENT BY GRAND JURY

Under the Fifth Amendment, the federal government cannot try anyone outside of the armed forces (the military, the navy, and the air force) for a serious federal crime without an indictment by a grand jury. (Those in the regular armed forces who are accused of federal crimes are tried in military courts.) An indictment is a formal document that accuses someone or a group of people of a crime, a serious illegal act that is seen as affecting the public, although only one person might have been harmed. Examples of crimes are murder, arson, burglary, and robbery.

A grand jury is a group of people chosen to examine the government's accusations against someone charged with (formally accused of) a crime. The Fifth Amendment also says that a grand jury can make a presentment. A presentment is like an indictment, except that the members of a grand jury make a presentment by choice, without an indictment laid before them; or, they make a presentment based on their own knowledge. The grand jury clause was meant to protect people against careless, groundless, or mean-spirited charges by the government. In *Hurtado v. California* (1884), the U.S. Supreme Court said that the Fifth Amendment does not require the states to use grand juries.

Origins of the Grand Jury

The grand jury has roots in ancient Athens, Greece; England under the Anglo-Saxons (Germanic peoples who conquered England in the fifth century); and England's King Henry II's Assize of Clarendon of 1166. The Assize of Clarendon was a series of laws begun by Henry II that established the grand jury. The Grand Assize, as the jury was called, was made up of local gentry (those who were socially ranked below nobles but above small landowning farmers). The Grand Assize consisted of 12 men in each 100, and four men in each township. Members of the Grand Assize, relying on first-hand accounts and rumor, were supposed to report to the king's traveling judges the most serious crimes and to name those accused and suspected of crimes. By the 17th century, the grand jury was seen as a safeguard against unjust charges by the government.

The Grand Jury System

In the modern-day grand jury system in the United States, the prosecutor presents the indictment before a grand jury. Prosecutors are lawyers who, on behalf of the government, formally accuse someone suspected of a crime and try to prove in court that the accused is guilty. In other words, prosecutors prosecute those suspected of crimes. If the grand jury believes that the prosecutor has presented enough evidence to justify a trial, the grand jury approves the indictment. Grand juries also have the power to investigate: They are often chosen to make investigations and issue reports.

Grand juries differ from trial juries in many ways. First, unlike trial juries, grand juries do not decide whether the accused is guilty. Second, grand juries usually have many more members than trial juries, which usually have 12 members. Grand juries usually have between 12 and 23 members. Federal grand juries usually have between 16 and 23 members.

Third, in jury trials, two opposing sides, usually represented by lawyers, present evidence to the jury by questioning witnesses. In grand jury proceedings, however, prosecutors do most or all of the questioning of witnesses, whereas, potential defendants or their lawyers cannot call witnesses at all. Moreover, prosecutors do not have to present both sides of the case.

Fourth, prosecutors can also introduce evidence that a judge might not allow them to present in a jury trial. Moreover, prosecutors do not have to follow the exclusionary rule: They can base their questioning of witnesses on evidence that was obtained illegally.

Fifth, grand jury witnesses do not have the same rights as trial witnesses. For example, grand jury witnesses can be forced to testify (make a statement under oath). They also cannot bring lawyers with them into the grand jury room. Grand jury witnesses also do not have to be told whether they may be indicted. Finally, unlike jury trials, grand jury proceedings are "closed," or secret. The USA PATRIOT Act, however, allows certain federal officials to receive information involving foreign intelligence from grand jury proceedings.

Many people believe that grand juries serve mostly prosecutors, not the accused. Grand juries tend to indict when prosecutors advise them to indict. The secrecy of grand jury proceedings also makes abuses by prosecutors more likely. For example, secrecy enables prosecutors to trick and bully witnesses, or to mislead grand jurors.

Today, most states in the United States do not require a prosecutor to issue an indictment. Instead, they allow a prosecutor to issue an information (a written accusation of a crime), which does not have to be approved by a grand jury.

THE RIGHT
AGAINST DOUBLE JEOPARDY

When an accused person is tried for a crime, he or she is in *jeopardy* (that is, in danger) of being punished. *Double jeopardy* means the trying of someone twice for the same crime (thereby, putting that person in the same danger twice). The Fifth Amendment bars double jeopardy whether the person was acquitted (found not guilty) or convicted. The amendment also forbids the government from punishing someone twice for the same crime. In 1959, however, the Court said in *Abbate v. United States* and *Bartkus v. Illinois* that the federal government and a state government can prosecute the same defendant for the same crime. As a matter of policy, however, the federal government avoids prosecuting a case that has already been prosecuted by a state.

The double jeopardy clause was meant to prevent the government from repeatedly exposing someone to the risks connected with being tried for a crime. For example, someone accused of a crime risks losing his or her job, reputation, or (if found guilty) freedom or life. Also, defending oneself against criminal charges can cost a lot of time and money. The phrase "jeopardy of life or limb," which comes from common law, used to refer generally to the risk of capital punishment (the risk of being put to death) if found guilty. In *Ex parte Lange* (1874), however, the U.S. Supreme Court denied that jeopardy must involve risk to "life or limb." (*Ex parte* means that the case involved one side.)

The right against double jeopardy has roots in ancient Greek, Roman, and Roman Catholic Church law. English common law allowed defendants to plead former acquittal or former conviction (to state that they had been acquitted of the crime or convicted) in order to prevent a retrial. In colonial and revolutionary America, the common law rule that defendants can claim double jeopardy only if they were convicted or acquitted in the first trial was followed in some cases. In other cases, the rule against double jeopardy was understood as barring a second trial even if the accused was neither convicted nor acquitted in the first trial.

THE RIGHT AGAINST SELF-INCRIMINATION

To incriminate someone is to accuse that person of being involved in a crime, or to show evidence or proof that he or she is involved in a crime. Self-incrimination is the act of incriminating oneself. Most people have probably heard or seen someone "plead the Fifth" in a courtroom or a hearing. People who plead the Fifth are exercising their Fifth Amendment right against self-incrimination (or the right not to accuse themselves): That is, they are saying that they will not answer a question because to do so truthfully might suggest that they had been or are involved in a crime. Witnesses and the accused have the right against self-incrimination. In *Counselman v. Hitchcock* (1892), the U.S. Supreme Court said that the Fifth Amendment also guarantees witnesses the right against self-incrimination in federal grand jury proceedings. In *Quinn v. United States* (1955), the Court said that the Fifth Amendment guarantees witnesses the right against self-incrimination in legislative investigations. In *McCarthy v. Arndstein* (1924), the Court also extended the right to civil cases if answering truthfully places the person at risk of being prosecuted for a crime or punished. (Civil cases are noncriminal cases, for example, those involving legal disagreements between individuals.)

On the other hand, to get evidence concerning a crime, the government can force a witness to testify by granting him or her immunity from prosecution. That is to say, in return for the witness's testimony, the government promises not to use the witness's testimony against him or her in a trial. Immunity, in this case, means freedom from being punished for a crime. The government can still, however, put the witness on trial with evidence unrelated to the witness's testimony. In some cases, a state government promises a witness that the government will not try to punish him or her under any circumstances for the crime. The federal government, however, does not grant this type of immunity.

> "The Fifth Amendment is an old friend and a good friend. It is one of the great landmarks in man's struggle to be free of tyranny, to be decent and civilized. It is our way of escape from the use of torture."
>
> —William O. Douglas, associate justice of the U.S. Supreme Court (1939–75), An Almanac of Liberty, 1954

Origins

The American right against self-incrimination comes largely from the English common law system of criminal justice. The source of the Fifth Amendment clause is the maxim "no man is bound to accuse himself." The right resulted from the conflict between two systems of justice: the accusatorial system (used by English common law courts) and the inquisitorial system (developed by English church courts and used also by other royal courts, which were not bound by common law).

Before people could be proven guilty of a crime in the accusatorial system, they first had to be accused of a crime; then, they had to be tried publicly by a judge. In the inquisitorial system, the judge examined the facts and questioned witnesses. In England during the 16th and 17th centuries, the judge, under this system, was also the accuser and the prosecutor. The English inquisitorial system during this period also allowed torture to force confessions. Common law courts also tried to force those accused or suspected of crimes to incriminate themselves. The accusatorial system, however, was fairer to the accused. Moreover, common law courts never approved torture, although the Crown held the right to use torture until 1641.

Church courts used inquisitions especially in order to discover and punish nonconformists (those whose religious views and teachings did not agree with the teachings of the Church of England). In church courts, officials forced the accused to take an oath (referred to as the oath *ex officio*) to answer all questions as truthfully and as fully as possible. Before taking the oath, the accused were not told the charges against them, what they were going to be asked, or whether they were even accused of a crime. The royal court of the Star Chamber also used the oath *ex officio*. In the early 16th century, the Court of Star Chamber (so called because of the stars painted on the ceiling) became a means to suppress political dissenters. Sentences (punishments ordered by a court) for those found guilty included whipping, branding (marking someone with a hot iron), and pillorying (placing someone in a public place with his or her hands and head locked in the holes of a wooden frame). The court, however, never sentenced anyone to death.

Puritans often had to face the oath *ex officio*. Puritanism arose around 1560 as a movement to reform the Church of England, which Puritans believed was too much like the Roman Catholic Church. (King Henry VIII had broken the English church away from the Catholic Church of Rome in 1534.) The early Puritans believed that Scripture did not support the Church of England's worship practices or the setting up of bishops and churches by the government. By the 17th century, the Crown was oppressing Puritans for their religious beliefs. Suspected nonconformists were summoned before the Court of High Commission, which exercised power over church matters on behalf of the Crown. The Commission relied on the oath *ex officio,* not torture, to get answers. Those who refused to take the oath or to answer questions after taking the oath were sentenced for contempt (refusal to obey or respect a court or a judge) and were likely to be tried in the court of the Star Chamber.

Legislative Investigations

After World War II (1939–45), the United States, the Soviet Union, and their allies became rivals. During this struggle, known as the cold war, the two superpowers avoided a direct war, although each country engaged in combat to keep allies from changing sides or to overthrow allies that had done so. The Soviet Union's system of government was much different from that of the United States. The Soviet Union's system of government was based on communism, a system where the government or the community, not individuals, owns property and controls how and what goods are produced, and who gets which goods. In the Soviet Union, the government, under the control of the Communist Party, owned property and controlled the economy. The United States has a capitalist system, where the government interferes less in the economy. Moreover, the theories on which communism (Soviet-style communism) is based call for the overthrow of capitalism. The cold war ended with the fall of the Soviet Union in 1991.

In 1946 and 1950, concerns about the increased power of the Soviet Union, the spread of communism across the world, the confessions of former American Communists, and cases of Communist spying prompted government agencies to investigate the threat of Communism in the United States. The U.S. Senate gave two of its committees power to investigate communism in the United States: the Judiciary Committee's Subcommittee on Internal Security and the Government Operations Committee's Subcommittee on Investigations. These committees held hearings where the committees called people to testify about their ties or those of others to Communist organizations. The U.S. House of Representatives' House Un-

JOHN LILBURNE
(ca. 1614–1657)

Puritan activist John Lilburne did a lot to make the right against self-incrimination a rule of common law. In 1637, Lilburne was arrested for smuggling Puritan pamphlets into England. When he went before the court of the Star Chamber for trial, he refused to take the oath *ex officio*. In 1638, Lilburne was found guilty, fined, publicly whipped, pilloried, and imprisoned. Lilburne's refusal to take the oath focused a lot of public attention on the injustice of forcing people to incriminate themselves. In December 1640, the English Parliament freed Lilburne from prison. In 1641, Parliament, which was controlled by the Puritan party and common lawyers (lawyers who specialize in the common law), denounced the sentences against Lilburne and others, ended the Star Chamber and the High Commission, and banned church officials from giving any oath that required takers of the oath to incriminate themselves in a crime.

When Parliament arrested and questioned him in 1645, Lilburne unsuccessfully claimed the right against self-incrimination. In doing so, he became the first hostile witness to claim a right not to answer in-criminating questions in an investigation by a legislature. He also claimed the right before a common law court in 1649, when he was tried for treason (the crime of trying to overthrow the government or of helping a country's enemies in war). He argued that Magna Carta and the Petition of Right guaranteed him the right against self-incrimination. The London jury acquitted him.

Lilburne, however, was again tried for treason, for which he was again acquitted in 1653. The government, however, believing him to be dangerous, kept Lilburne in prison until 1655. By this time, he had become a Quaker. He died two years later.

Before he died, Lilburne had stood trial for his life four times and spent most of the last 20 years of his life in jail, where he smuggled out countless political pamphlets. After Lilburne's death, the right against self-incrimination gradually became established in English law. By the early 18th century, those accused of crimes could no longer be witnesses for or against themselves, even if they wanted to. The accused was allowed to tell his or her own story, but not under oath.

American Activities Committee (HUAC), created in 1938 to investigate disloyalty and organizations that sought the overthrow of the U.S. government, also focused on exposing American Communists and Communist ideas and information in American society. Some

Martin Dies, Jr., Democratic representative from Texas, from 1931 to 1945 and 1951 to 1959, was the first chairman of the House Un-American Activities Committee. *(Library of Congress, Prints and Photographs Division [LC-USZ62-118238])*

government agencies did find actual cases where Communists had gained government positions. The committees' often reckless and unproven charges, however, ruined the careers of countless innocent people.

Critics of the committees' anti-Communist investigations argued that they violated the civil liberties of witnesses. (A civil liberty is the freedom to do something without meddling by the government or someone else. For example, the freedom to speak one's mind is a civil liberty.) Some witnesses refused to answer questions, some justifying their refusal on the Fifth Amendment right against self-incrimination. (Others justified their refusal on the First Amendment.) Many witnesses were charged with contempt for refusing to answer questions. In *Quinn, Emspak v. United States,* and *Bart v. United States* (which the U.S. Supreme Court decided together in 1955), all of the justices agreed that witnesses before legislative committees can claim the Fifth Amendment right against self-incrimination.

The Right to Remain Silent

Before 1966, someone being questioned by the police had to claim the right against self-incrimination if he or she wanted to be protected by the right. As interpreted by earlier U.S. Supreme Court decisions, the self-incrimination clause did not bar unforced confessions or other incriminating statements from being used as evidence in trials. Also, police officers did not have to warn suspects that they had a right not to answer questions. Moreover, suspects did not have the right to have a lawyer present during police questioning. In *Miranda v. Arizona* (1966), the Court said that police questioning was by its nature coercive and, therefore, contrary to the Fifth Amendment's self-incrimination clause. To ensure that suspects who made incriminating statements did so voluntarily, the Court in *Miranda* required police officers to inform suspects that are under arrest that they have the right to remain silent and to have a lawyer present during questioning.

Miranda involved the case of Ernesto Miranda. On March 13, 1963, in Phoenix, Arizona, officers arrested Miranda at his home

JOSEPH R. McCARTHY
(1908–1957)

On February 9, 1950, in a speech in Wheeling, West Virginia, U.S. senator Joseph R. McCarthy held up a piece of paper and claimed that it was a list of 205 Communists working in the U.S. State Department. That speech changed the little-known Republican senator from Wisconsin into a nationally known politician. A Senate investigating committee later concluded that McCarthy's charges, which McCarthy never supported with any evidence, were a hoax. Nevertheless, McCarthy repeated his accusations on radio and television, winning popular support by taking advantage of Americans' fear of communism.

After being reelected in 1952, McCarthy became chairman of the Senate Permanent Subcommittee on Investigations. As chairman, McCarthy held well-publicized hearings where he investigated government departments and questioned countless witnesses about their connections to communism. McCarthy's accusations, based on flimsy evidence, ruined many careers and reputations. McCarthy even questioned the integrity of President Dwight D. Eisenhower (U.S. president from 1953 to 1961) and other leaders of the Republican and Democratic parties.

McCarthy's tactics finally led to his downfall. In 1954, in a nationally televised 36-day hearing, he accused the secretary of the U.S. Army and his aides of trying to hide evidence of disloyalty at an army base. After seeing McCarthy on television bullying witnesses and making unsupported charges, the public turned against him. After the Democrats gained control of the Senate in the midterm elections in November 1954, the Senate replaced McCarthy as chairman of the Subcommittee on Investigations. On December 2, 1954, the U.S. Senate voted 67 to 22 to condemn McCarthy for conduct "contrary to Senate traditions." During the rest of his life, McCarthy was largely ignored as a political figure, and he quickly became an alcoholic. He died on May 2, 1957, in Bethesda, Maryland, of a disease of the liver at age 48. Publicly attacking someone's loyalty or character with flimsy or no evidence became known as McCarthyism.

Joseph R. McCarthy was a U.S. senator from Wisconsin from 1947 to 1957. *(Library of Congress, Prints and Photographs Division [LC-USZ62-94487])*

and took him to the Phoenix police station. There, a rape victim identified Miranda from a lineup as her attacker. A *lineup* is a group of people and a suspect arranged in a line, organized especially to see whether a witness to a crime can identify the suspect. Police officers then took Miranda, a poor Mexican immigrant, to a room where two police officers questioned him. Two hours later, the officers came out of the room holding a written confession signed by Miranda. As stated in the Court opinion, "At the top of the statement was a typed paragraph stating that the confession was made voluntarily, without threats or promises of immunity, and 'with full knowledge of my legal rights, understanding any statement I make may be used against me.'" The officers later admitted during the trial that they had not warned Miranda that he had a

This photo shows the Burger Court in 1976. *Miranda v. Arizona* (1966) was one of the most controversial decisions by the U.S. Supreme Court under Chief Justice Earl Warren. The Court under Chief Justice Warren E. Burger eased some of the limits on law enforcement officers regarding *Miranda* rules. *(Library of Congress, Prints and Photographs Division [LC-USZ62-60135])*

right to have a lawyer present during the questioning. Also, although one of the officers testified that he had read this paragraph to Miranda, the officer apparently did not do so until after Miranda had confessed orally. Miranda's confession was used against him during the trial. Miranda was convicted of kidnapping and rape and sentenced to 20 to 30 years in prison.

In 1966, the Court reversed Miranda's conviction. *Miranda* was one of four cases that the Court decided together. The Court said that prosecutors cannot use statements that defendants make during police questioning unless prosecutors can show that steps had been followed to protect the right of defendants against self-incrimination. The Court also outlined a set of warnings that the police must give people who have been arrested. Now, after arresting suspects, officers give suspects what are known as *Miranda* warnings, which advise people under arrest of their *Miranda* rights. Many people have seen television shows where a police officer warns someone that he or she has "the right to remain silent" and to have a lawyer present during questioning. A person can give up these rights, but the government must show that he or she did so voluntarily and intelligently before it can use the person's statements as evidence in a trial.

> "The Constitution requires that I inform you of your rights:
>
> "You have a right to remain silent. If you talk to any police officer, anything you say can and will be used against you in court.
>
> "You have a right to consult with a lawyer before you are questioned, and may have him with you during questioning.
>
> "If you cannot afford a lawyer, one will be appointed for you, if you wish, before any questioning.
>
> "If you wish to answer questions, you have the right to stop answering at any time.
>
> "You may stop answering questions at any time if you wish to talk to a lawyer, and may have him with you during any further questioning."
>
> —*an example of* Miranda *warnings*

The *Miranda* decision provoked harsh criticism. In his dissenting opinion, Justice Byron R. White warned, "In some unknown number of cases the Court's rule will return a killer, a rapist or other criminal to the streets and to the environment which produced him, to repeat his crime whenever it pleases him." Many probably agreed. The Court has since eased the limits *Miranda* placed on law enforcement officers. For example, in *New York v. Quarles* (1984), the Court said that a police officer does not have to give a suspect *Miranda* warnings before questioning if the officer is reasonably concerned for public safety.

THE RIGHT TO DUE PROCESS

Early in its history, the U.S. Supreme Court understood "deprived of life, liberty, or property" to simply mean *punished for a crime* and "due process of law" to simply mean legal actions that fairly and properly follow established rules and principles. This type of due process is called *procedural due process*. (A procedure is a series of steps followed in order.) In other words, the due process clause simply meant that the federal government had to follow fair and proper legal procedures before it could punish someone for a crime.

In time, the Court decided that laws that unfairly or unjustly affect someone's life, liberty, or property rights also violate due process. Thus, "due process of law" now also means substantive due process, which requires that laws involve a proper government interest and that they not result in unfair or unjust treatment of individuals. The Fifth Amendment's due process clause limits the federal government. The Fourteenth Amendment's due process clause, taken nearly word for word from the Fifth's, imposes the same limits on the states.

Magna Carta

Magna Carta is considered the first document to guarantee the right to due process. In chapter 39 of Magna Carta (1215), the phrase "law of the land" essentially means a body of fundamental law. The belief that even the monarch must follow a higher law goes as far back as before the Middle Ages (from 500 to 1500 A.D.). As early as the 14th century, however, the phrase "law of the land" was also understood to mean fair and proper legal procedures.

When Magna Carta was revised for the third time in 1225, chapter 29 of this version restated chapter 39 of the original. A 1354 act of Parliament restating chapter 29 replaced "law of the land" with "due process of law." The 1354 act was the first document in English legal history to use this phrase. In the 1354 act, "due process of law" probably did not mean the same as "law of the land." In the act and until the 17th century, "due process of law" meant a proper common law writ. By the mid-17th century, "due process" and "law of the land" referred to procedural due process. The phrase "law of the land," however, was used most often, and "due process" continued to usually mean a proper common law writ.

Following the example of Magna Carta, American colonial charters most often used the phrase "law of the land." During the American Revolution, all of the first state constitutions restated chapter 39 of Magna Carta, using the phrase "law of the land." The U.S. Constitution was the first American constitution to use the phrase "due process of law," which to Americans, by this time, meant the same as "law of the land," or procedural due process.

Substantive Due Process and Discrimination

In *Bolling v. Sharpe* (1954), the U.S. Supreme Court applied the principle of substantive due process to the issue of discrimination (unfair or unequal treatment). In *Bolling,* the Court was asked to decide whether racial segregation (separation by race) of public schoolchildren in Washington, D.C., violated the due process clause of the Fifth Amendment.

Bolling involved the case of Spottswood Bolling, Jr., and African-American children in Washington, D.C., schools. In 1947, Gardner Bishop and the Consolidated Parents Group began a movement to end segregation in their schools. In 1950, Bishop tried to get 11 African-American children, including Bolling, admitted into the John Philip Sousa Junior High School. Bishop was angry that black students, like Bolling, were assigned to overcrowded, run-down schools, while white children were assigned nearby to the newly completed Sousa Junior High School. The school did not admit the children, even though the school had several empty classrooms.

The Court heard *Bolling* with the four cases now known as *Brown v. Board of Education* (1954). In *Brown,* the Court said that segregating children in state public schools by race violated the equal protection clause of the Fourteenth Amendment. The equal protection clause requires a state to treat a person or a group of people the same as the state treats

This photo shows Spottswood Bolling, Jr. (back row, right) during a press conference at the Hotel Americana, celebrating the 10th anniversary of *Brown v. Board of Education* (1954), which outlawed racial segregation in state public schools. The other three people shown *(left to right:* Linda Brown Smith, Harry Briggs, Jr., and Ethel Louise Belton) had brought three of the four cases that were decided in *Brown: Brown v. Board of Education of Topeka; Briggs v. Elliott; Davis v. County School Board of Prince Edward County, Virginia;* and *Gebhart v. Belton. (Library of Congress, Prints and Photographs Division [LC-USZ62-112705])*

other people or groups in the same or nearly the same circumstances. At the time of the *Brown* decision, 17 southern and border states and the District of Columbia required black and white elementary schoolchildren to attend different public schools. The Court gave a separate opinion on *Bolling v. Sharpe* because the Fourteenth Amendment applies only to the states, and thus not to the District of Columbia, a federal district.

The Court said that public school segregation in the District of Columbia violated the Fifth Amendment's due process clause, even though the amendment does not contain an equal protection clause. The Court stated that school segregation was "not reasonably related to any proper" government goal; therefore, barring black children from attending public schools attended by white children deprived black children of liberty without due process.

THE RIGHT TO JUST COMPENSATION

The just compensation clause recognizes the power of the government to take private property (whether or not the owner wants to give it) for public use. This is called the power of eminent domain. The clause, however, also requires the government to pay a fair price for property the government takes, and to take property only for public use. The U.S. Supreme Court interprets "just compensation" to mean the property's fair market value: The amount a willing buyer would pay a willing seller if the government did not want the property. For example, the property owner does not have the right to get more money because the government needs the property as soon as possible. Also, the government cannot pay less money because the government's plan for the property (for example, to build a federal prison) has made the property less valuable. The government must pay the property owner in cash right after taking the property.

The government takes property in other ways besides physically doing so. The government also "takes" property when the government does something that substantially deprives the property owner of his or her right to use or enjoy the property freely. For example, the Court considered this issue in *United States v. Causby* (1946). This case involved the flight of military planes just above a farm next to a military airport. The farm owners, who were husband and wife, used the farm mainly for raising chickens. Fright-

"The Fifth Amendment's guarantee that private property shall not be taken for a public use without just compensation was designed to bar Government from forcing some people alone to bear public burdens which, in all fairness and justice, should be borne by the public as a whole."

—*Associate Justice Hugo L. Black, delivering the opinion of the U.S. Supreme Court in* Armstrong v. United States *(1960)*

ened by the noise from the flights over the farm during takeoffs and landings, chickens would fly into the walls. About 150 chickens were killed this way. The noise made the farm nearly worthless for raising chickens. The farm owners claimed the farm had, in effect, been taken. The Court agreed and said that the owners were entitled to just compensation.

The Court has almost always decided that the government has taken property for public use. The Court has not interpreted "public use" to mean that the public must become the owner of the property. The public does not even have to benefit directly. Public use is any use that benefits the public at least generally. Also, in *Berman v. Parker* (1954), the Court allowed the federal government to give private corporations the power to take property when taking the property would promote a public purpose. For example, the federal government has taken private property and resold it to private companies to destroy slums and build low-cost housing. Federal and state governments have used their power to take private property for public use in order to help private companies do things like develop transportation, supply water to communities, create public parks, and preserve historic places.

4

The Right to a Fair Trial

In all criminal prosecutions, the accused shall enjoy the right to a speedy and public trial, by an impartial jury of the State and district wherein the crime shall have been committed, which district shall have been previously ascertained by law, and to be informed of the nature and cause of the accusation; to be confronted with the witnesses against him; to have compulsory process for obtaining witnesses in his favor, and to have the Assistance of Counsel for his defence.

—Amendment VI, Constitution of the United States

In suits at common law, where the value in controversy shall exceed twenty dollars, the right of trial by jury shall be preserved, and no fact tried by a jury, shall be otherwise reexamined in any Court of the United States, than according to the rules of the common law.

—Amendment VII, Constitution of the United States

The U.S. Constitution, in effect, guarantees defendants the right to a fair trial in the due process clauses of the Fifth and Fourteenth Amendments, which, together, require the federal government and the states to treat people fairly. The rights guaranteed by the Sixth Amendment are meant to help guarantee a fair trial. The Seventh Amendment guarantees defendants the right to trial by jury in federal civil cases.

THE RIGHT TO A SPEEDY TRIAL

The Sixth Amendment gives those accused of crimes the right to demand a speedy trial. The accused does not have to be indicted, or formally charged in some other way, before demanding a speedy trial if he or she was arrested beforehand. Guaranteeing the accused this right is meant to lessen the suffering that delaying a trial can cause defendants. For example, if the accused remains in jail, that person may lose his or her job or ties to family and friends. Even if the accused is free until the trial begins, the court may greatly limit what that person can do or where that person can go. The accused may lose a lot of money and time preparing for the trial. As time passes, preparing a good defense may become harder: For example, witnesses may die or forget facts. Also, the longer the accused waits, the more the accused may worry about whether he or she will be found guilty.

> "Our Law says well, to delay Justice is Injustice."
>
> —*William Penn (1644–1718), founder of Pennsylvania*, Some Fruits of Solitude, *in* Reflections and Maxims, *1693*

THE RIGHT TO A PUBLIC TRIAL

The Sixth Amendment's public trial clause was meant to prevent the government from using the courts to persecute people (that is, to hurt people because of, for example, their religious or political beliefs). The right to a public trial comes from English common law. Although exactly when the right appeared is unclear, the right to a public trial probably dates back to at least the 17th century, when the idea of jury trials as protection for those accused of crimes emerged in England. Some believe that British and American distrust of secret trials resulted from the abuse of secret trials by the Court of Star Chamber.

Besides helping to prevent trials from becoming a government weapon to persecute people, public trials also benefit society in other ways: For instance, a public trial helps to ensure that a defendant receives a fair trial and a fair and accurate verdict (jury decision). A public trial also discourages witnesses from lying, trial participants from acting illegally or unethically, and juries and judges from making biased decisions. A public trial also satisfies society's desire for revenge against those found guilty of serious crimes, such as murder.

Fair Trials and Freedom of the Press

The First Amendment's guarantee of freedom of the press also promotes public trials. Freedom of the press is the right to publish and spread information. In *Richmond Newspapers, Inc., v. Virginia* (1980), the U.S. Supreme Court said that, except in special cases,

> "Trial by television is . . . foreign to our system."
>
> —*Associate Justice Thomas C. Clark, delivering the opinion of the U.S. Supreme Court in* Estes v. Texas *(1965)*

the public and the press have the right under the First and Fourteenth Amendments to attend criminal trials and to get and publish information about them, even in cases where the accused would like to give up their right to a public trial. Thus, to grant a defendant's request for a closed trial, a judge would have to decide, by examining the facts, that publicity would probably harm the defendant's right to a fair trial and that closing the trial to the public would be the only way to protect that right.

Today, the mass media (newspapers, radio, television, and other forms of communication designed to reach a great number of people) regularly cover cases involving the rich, famous, and powerful, and people accused of sensational crimes, such as murder. The cable network Court TV broadcasts trials live during the week. Sometimes, however, the government must limit the freedom of the media to report on trials in order to ensure that a defendant has a fair trial.

For example, publicity about a case before a trial can make finding an unbiased jury harder or even impossible. Also, publicity during a trial can unfairly affect the jury's decision. The Court has sometimes reversed convictions in cases where it believed that local news reports biased jurors against defendants, or where jurors admitted that widespread reporting of the case had led them to assume from the beginning that the defendant was guilty. For example, in *Sheppard v. Maxwell* (1966), the Court said that excessive, biased publicity before and during the trial of a man later convicted of beating his wife to death had denied the defendant a fair trial. In *Chandler v. Florida* (1981), however, the Court said that states can allow television cameras, photo cameras, and radio microphones in the courtroom as long as the media can report the news without denying the defendant a fair trial.

THE RIGHT TO TRIAL BY JURY

In criminal trials, defendants have the right to be tried by a jury, although they can choose to have a judge decide whether they are guilty or not guilty. Trial juries are called petit juries. The jury trial clause was meant to help protect those who may be charged unjustly purely for political reasons. The clause was also meant to protect the accused against judges who may be biased in favor of the government. In *Baldwin v. New York* (1970), however, the U.S. Supreme Court said that the U.S. Constitution does not require trial by jury in state trials for those accused of petty crimes (minor crimes that carry a sentence of no more than six months).

Origins of Jury Trials

Historians disagree about when and where the English trial jury began. Some trace it to the times of the Anglo-Saxons, or even earlier. Some believe that King Alfred the Great of England started the jury system in the ninth century. Most historians, however, believe that the Normans (people from Normandy, a region in northwestern France) brought the jury system to England when they conquered the country in 1066. The Norman period in England ended in 1154. Originally, jurors were neighbors who had personal knowledge of the case in question.

This photo shows the trial of George Jacobs, Sr., on August 5, 1692. Jacobs was hanged for practicing witchcraft on August 19, 1692. His trial was one of a series of trials in the village of Salem, Massachusetts, known as the "Salem Witch Trials." *(Library of Congress, Prints and Photographs Division [LC-USZ62-94432])*

TRIAL BY ORDEAL

During the Middle Ages throughout Europe, before trial by jury became common in England, one's guilt or innocence was often decided by trial by ordeal, in which the accused would perform a test. The outcome, believed to reveal divine will, would decide whether the accused was innocent or guilty. One common form of ordeal was trial by fire, in which the accused walked through fire or put his or her hand into a flame. Another form of ordeal called for the accused to plunge his or her hand into hot, melted metal. The common belief was that God would protect the innocent.

Trial by water was used to find out whether a woman was a witch. The accused was bound and thrown into water that had been blessed. If she floated, she was found guilty (because the water had "rejected" her). If the water "accepted" her (that is, if she sank), she was found innocent.

When the Normans conquered England in 1066, royal judges appointed by Norman kings introduced the Saxon tradition of trial by battle. In this trial, the two sides in a dispute would fight to resolve the issue, which would be decided in favor of the win-ner. A woman, child, or man too weak to fight for himself could have a champion. Champions were knights who had agreed to fight for those who could not fight for themselves.

Trial by wager of law was another form of ordeal the Normans adopted from the Saxons. In trials by wager of law, both sides had to ask their neighbors to serve as oath helpers, those who would be willing to swear to the good character of someone on one side of the dispute. Each side had to try to get more oath helpers than the other. Because they were willing to risk salvation by standing up as a group for one side or the other, oath helpers were believed to express divine will.

In 1215, the Roman Catholic Church forbade priests and other officials of the Church from participating in trials by ordeal. This made the outcomes of trials by ordeal look less like expressions of divine will. Trials by ordeal disappeared in England and on the European continent by the mid-13th century. Trials by ordeal still existed in many parts of Asia and Africa until recent times.

Starting in the mid-12th century, the earliest role of juries in cases concerning crimes was to present accusations, not to decide questions of guilt or innocence. (In other words, they were what are now called grand jurors.) Later, jurors answered on oath the question of guilt or innocence. Such oaths, however, were unsupported by evidence. Also, to reverse an improper verdict, a second jury had to be willing to swear that the first jury had knowingly given a false verdict. Because the first jury could be punished for giving a false verdict, juries, understandably, rarely wanted to cause other juries to be punished.

In 1194, accusatory and trial juries (the grand and petit juries of today) became separate forms. Trials by petit jury were used in Norman royal courts during the 13th century. By the 16th century, trial by petit jury had become the established way to try criminal and civil cases at common law. In the early 15th century, judges of the courts of common law restricted the jury to judging questions of fact based on evidence submitted during trial. During the 17th century, trial by jury became regarded as a way to protect the accused. Also, in the 17th century, prosecuting a jury for giving a false verdict was gradually replaced by granting a new trial when the first verdict seemed to be unsupported by most of the evidence. A new trial could be granted for this reason in criminal and civil cases, except when doing so would violate rules against double jeopardy.

Criminal Cases

Besides being in the Bill of Rights, the right to trial by jury in federal criminal cases is in Article 3, Section 2 of the U.S. Constitution. A trial jury is a group of usually 12 people who decide whether the accused is guilty or not guilty. In a jury trial, the jury usually decides only questions of fact. That is, the jury reaches its decision by looking at the evidence. The judge usually decides only questions of law. For example, the judge decides whether the defense or the prosecutor can present certain evidence in court, instructs the jury on law that applies to the case, and decides whether the questions a lawyer asks a witness are proper. Also, the Sixth Amendment requires that the jury be impartial. This means that the jurors must not be for or against one side or the other: They must decide the case based only on the evidence presented at trial. If the jury finds the defendant guilty, the judge declares the sentence. In some districts, the jury sets the sentence.

In federal criminal cases, all the jurors must agree on the verdict. The U.S. Supreme Court, however, has allowed majority decisions in state trials. In *Johnson v. Louisiana* (1972), a case involving a conviction based on a verdict agreed to by nine of 12 jurors, the Court said that a conviction based on a verdict agreed to by fewer than all the members of a jury in a state criminal trial does not violate the due process and equal protection clauses of the Fourteenth Amendment. In *Apodaca v. Oregon,* which the Court decided together with *Johnson,* the Court said that a conviction based on a 10-2 verdict in a state criminal trial did not violate the defendant's right to a trial by jury under the Sixth and Fourteenth Amendments.

The Sixth Amendment also requires that, in federal cases, the jury be "of the State and district wherein the crime shall have been committed." This means that, in federal cases, the jury must be drawn from the district of the state where the crime occurred. A district is a division of the state where the court has the power to hear the case. In *Nashville, Chattanooga, & St. Louis Railway Co. v.*

THE TWELVE-PERSON JURY

By tradition, a criminal trial jury in the United States is usually made up of 12 people. In the United States, the 12-person jury is rooted in English common law. In England, for unclear reasons, the number of jurors on a petit jury was fixed at 12 during the 14th century. The practice of using 12 jurors was also widely used in other European countries since early times. Some historians believe that the number had religious and mystical meaning. For example, the Bible tells of the 12 tribes of Israel and the 12 followers of Jesus.

Until its decision in *Patton v. United States* (1930), the U.S. Supreme Court assumed that the U.S. Constitution required juries in federal criminal cases to have 12 people. In *Patton,* however, the Court said that in a federal criminal trial, a defendant could agree to have a jury of only 11 or 10 members if the prosecutor and the judge also agreed. In *Williams v. Florida* (1970), the Court said that a jury of only six people in a state trial concerning a serious crime did not violate the Constitution. Later, the Court said in *Ballew v. Georgia* (1978) that a jury of five people was too small. In *Burch v. Louisiana* (1979), the Court said that in a state trial concerning a nonpetty crime, a conviction based on a 5-1 verdict by a six-person jury violated the defendant's right to trial by jury under the Sixth and Fourteenth Amendments.

"Juries are not qualified to *judge* questions of *law,* but they are very capable of judging questions of *fact.*"

—*Thomas Jefferson, in a letter to M. L'Abbé Arnoud, July 19, 1789*

Alabama (1888), the Court said that the Sixth Amendment does not require the courts in state trials to draw the jury from the district where the crime happened. State courts, however, have generally

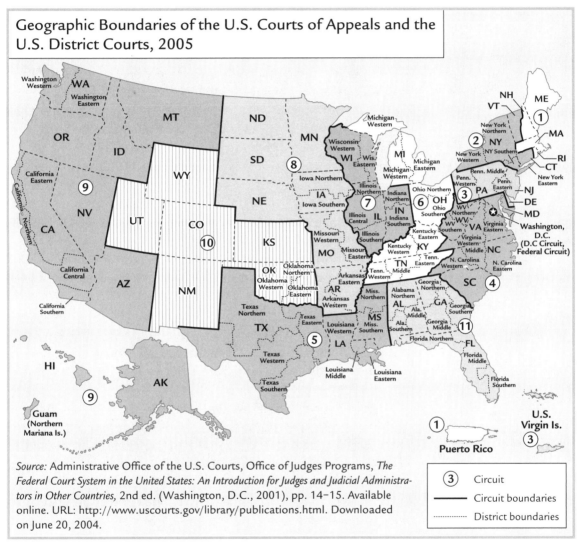

Geographic Boundaries of the U.S. Courts of Appeals and the U.S. District Courts, 2005

Source: Administrative Office of the U.S. Courts, Office of Judges Programs, *The Federal Court System in the United States: An Introduction for Judges and Judicial Administrators in Other Countries,* 2nd ed. (Washington, D.C., 2001), pp. 14–15. Available online. URL: http://www.uscourts.gov/library/publications.html. Downloaded on June 20, 2004.

The Sixth Amendment requires that, in a federal jury trial, the court draw the jury from the district where the crime happened. This map shows the districts of the U.S. federal courts. There are 94 federal trial court districts and 12 circuits, each of which has a U.S. court of appeals. Appeals are cases that are taken by one side in a case to a higher court for review in order to try to convince the court that the lower court made an error in law. Also, there is the Court of Appeals for the Federal Circuit, which has nationwide power to hear certain cases.

drawn juries from areas as small as the county where the crime occurred.

Civil Cases

The Seventh Amendment was meant to preserve the right to trial by jury in civil cases as the right existed at the time under English common law. In the Seventh Amendment, *suits* refers to civil cases. Civil cases are noncriminal cases and mostly involve private rights. A common example of a civil case is one where a property owner sues (brings a case against) someone for damaging the owner's property. Another example is one where someone sues a company for creating unsafe conditions that caused him or her to be injured. The person bringing the civil case is called the *plaintiff*. The person against whom the plaintiff is bringing the civil case is called the *defendant*. The plaintiff sues the defendant because the plaintiff wants the defendant to make up for the plaintiff's loss or to right the wrong done to the plaintiff. A plaintiff or a defendant can also be a group (such as a corporation).

If a plaintiff wins a civil case, the judge awards damages. *Damages* are the money that a court orders the losing side to pay the winning side in order to make up for the winning side's loss or injury. In some districts, the jury awards damages. In most cases, the judge has the power to lower, but not raise, the amount of damages awarded by a jury. Also, the plaintiff, the defense, or both can ask the judge to decide against the verdict or the amount of the award.

In the Seventh Amendment, the phrase "suits at common law" refers to cases where English common law recognized the right to trial by jury. For example, unlike common law courts, British vice-admiralty courts (which decided cases involving conduct, travel, and trade on the seas) did not use juries: In these courts, a judge, who was appointed by the Crown, decided questions of law and fact.

When the Americans were still British colonists, the British government tried Americans accused of violating the Stamp Act in vice-admiralty courts. Passed by the British Parliament in 1765, the act required that all newspapers, pamphlets, legal documents, advertisements, and other papers issued in the American colonies bear a stamp, which the colonists had to buy from the British gov-

CLASS ACTION SUITS

Sometimes, a group of people may wish to sue a private organization, a private company, or a government for harming a large class of people or for violating the rights of those who belong to that class. A *class* is a group that is alike in some way. For example, a group of older workers who work for the same company may wish to sue it as a class for paying older workers less than younger workers. A group of people who bought the same type of car may wish to sue the carmaker as a class for selling unsafe cars that have caused death or injury. In such cases, where a large class of people has been harmed or treated unfairly, not everyone who belongs to the group can join in the lawsuit. In such cases, federal and most state courts sometimes allow a group of people to bring a class action, in which a much smaller group of people sue on behalf of a large class of people. In most types of class action suits, all members of the class are bound by the outcome of the suit, unless one of the members chooses to exclude himself or herself at the beginning of the lawsuit.

Groups have used class action suits to bring about changes in society. For example, African-American schoolchildren (through their parents) have sued school officials to change policies that, the plaintiffs claim, discriminate against children according to race.

ernment. Reacting to pressure from British merchants, whose businesses were suffering because Americans were refusing to buy their goods, Parliament ended the Stamp Act in 1766.

Although the colonists had been more upset by the tax (which, they argued, violated their right against taxation without representation), they also complained that trying colonists in vice-admiralty courts for not paying the stamp tax or not using taxed paper violated the colonists' right to trial by jury, because the fate of the accused rested solely in the hands of judges appointed by the Crown.

The last clause in the Seventh Amendment says that "no fact tried by a jury, shall be otherwise reexamined in any Court of the

Anti-Federalist Elbridge Gerry (1744–1814) opposed adopting the U.S. Constitution for not including, among other rights, the right to trial by jury in civil cases. *(Library of Congress, Prints and Photographs Division [LC-USZ62-111790])*

United States, than according to the rules of the common law." The clause was meant to keep the roles of juries and courts separate, as they were under English common law: Except for cases where defendants voluntarily give up their right to trial by jury, juries decide questions of fact; judges decide questions of law. The first Congress under the U.S. Constitution added this clause to quiet fears that the powers of the U.S. Supreme Court (which, under Article 3 of the Constitution, has the power to decide questions of law and fact) threatened the common law right to trial by jury in civil cases. The last clause in the Seventh Amendment limits the power of the Court to review jury decisions in federal civil cases.

THE RIGHT TO KNOW THE CHARGES

The Sixth Amendment requires that the accused be told what they are accused of doing. The accused is notified of the charges so that he or she may answer the charges and, if the accused pleads not guilty, prepare for trial. After being formally charged, the accused must either accept or deny the charges. Knowing exactly what they are accused of doing also enables defendants to protect themselves against double jeopardy.

The Sixth Amendment does not specify how the accused is to be informed of the accusation, or who or what institution must notify the accused. These questions, however, have been settled by other sections of the Constitution, by past practice, and by judges' opinions. In federal felony cases, for instance, the Fifth Amendment requires that the accused be indicted by a grand jury. (Felonies are crimes that are punishable by a heavy sentence, such as over a year in prison or death, because they are considered to be more serious than other types of crimes.) For less serious federal crimes, a prosecutor need only issue an information; sometimes, even a complaint will do. (A *complaint* is a document, sworn to by a victim or a police officer, charging someone with a crime.) The courts have also required that indictments and information show that the accused is not being put in double jeopardy.

THE RIGHT TO CONFRONT AND CALL WITNESSES

The right to confront witnesses and the right to have compulsory process deal with the right of the accused to get evidence from trial witnesses. The right of the accused to confront the witnesses against them means that the accused have the right at trial to question the witnesses against them face to face. This right gives the accused the chance to challenge a witness and to force him or her to face the jurors so that they may judge whether the witness is believable.

The Sixth Amendment's compulsory process clause gives the accused the right to call upon the government to force someone to appear in court and to testify as a witness for the defense. "Compulsory process" refers to the legal means used to force someone to appear in court in order to testify as a witness for the defense. A well-known example of a compulsory process is the *subpoena,* a written court order to someone to appear in court. The order warns that the person will be punished if he or she fails to appear. There are two types of subpoenas: One type orders someone to appear in court and testify as a witness. Another orders someone to bring before the court documents or evidence named on the subpoena. The defense can use the same legal means that the prosecutor can use to make sure witnesses appear in court.

THE RIGHT TO A LAWYER

The Sixth Amendment guarantees the accused the right to have a lawyer. Whether the framers of the U.S. Constitution meant the right to counsel to include the right of poor defendants to be assigned lawyers in criminal cases is unclear. Until the 20th century, however, the right was generally assumed to mean the right to hire a lawyer for one's defense, not the right to be assigned a lawyer.

In *Johnson v. Zerbst* (1938), the U.S. Supreme Court said that poor defendants have the right to be given a lawyer in federal criminal cases. Concerning state criminal cases, however, the Court said in *Betts v. Brady* (1942) that not providing lawyers for poor defendants in noncapital cases did not deny them a fair trial,

"No system worth preserving should have to fear that if an accused is permitted to consult with a lawyer, he will become aware of, and exercise, these rights."

—*Associate Justice Arthur J. Goldberg, delivering the opinion of the U.S. Supreme Court in* Escobedo v. Illinois *(1964)*

> "This noble idea [of a fair trial] cannot be realized if the poor man charged with crime has to face his accusers without a lawyer to assist him."
>
> —*Associate Justice Hugo L. Black, delivering the opinion of the U.S. Supreme Court in* Gideon v. Wainwright *(1963)*

as required by due process of law under the Fourteenth Amendment. The Court said that states have to provide poor defendants a lawyer in serious state criminal cases only when special circumstances seriously hurt the defendants' ability to defend themselves. Examples of such circumstances are those where the charges against the accused are complex; or where the accused are young, mentally ill, or unable to read. Nearly 21 years later, however, the Court changed its mind. In 1963, the Court said in *Gideon v. Wainwright* that poor defendants have the right to be given a lawyer in state criminal cases. Most important, for the first time, the Court said that the right to a lawyer is fundamental to a fair trial.

Gideon involved the case of Clarence Earl Gideon. In 1961, Gideon was charged with breaking into and entering the Bay Harbor Poolroom in Panama City, Florida, and stealing a pint of wine and change from a cigarette machine. Gideon was a drifter and a petty thief who had already served time in prison four times. When he went to trial, Gideon, who was too poor to hire a lawyer, asked the judge to assign him a lawyer. The judge denied his request since the laws of Florida required the state to assign lawyers to the accused only in capital cases. Gideon was convicted.

In his petition to the Court, Gideon claimed that Florida had violated a Court rule that defendants in felony cases have a lawyer. Gideon was wrong. The rule at the time was that due process did not require poor defendants to have a lawyer in all state felony cases. After accepting Gideon's case, the Court appointed Abe Fortas, one of the best lawyers in Washington, D.C., to represent Gideon. Fortas later became a justice on the Court. Reversing its previous position, the Court declared in *Gideon* that the right to a lawyer in criminal cases is "fundamental and essential" to a fair trial. After the Court's decision, Gideon was tried again in Bay County, Florida; this time, represented by a lawyer, he was acquitted.

Hugo L. Black, associate justice of the U.S. Supreme Court from 1937 to 1971, delivered the decision in *Gideon v. Wainwright* (1963), which required the states to assign lawyers to poor defendants in state trials. *(Library of Congress, Prints and Photographs Division [LC-USZ62-95031])*

5

The Right Against Excessive or Cruel and Unusual Punishments

Excessive bail shall not be required, nor excessive fines imposed, nor cruel and unusual punishments inflicted.

—Amendment VIII, Constitution of the United States

The Eighth Amendment forbids the government from imposing excessive bail. Before a prisoner's trial, the government sometimes releases the prisoner from prison temporarily in return for bail, money that is put up or promised in return for the prisoner's release. The court demands bail to ensure that the prisoner will appear before the court at the required time. Bail can be cash, property, the bond of someone of means, or the bond bought from a professional bondsperson or bonding company. (A bond is a written agreement where someone or a company agrees to put up the prisoner's bail, or where someone or a company promises to pay the bail if the prisoner does not return when agreed.) If the prisoner appears as agreed, the money can be reclaimed. Otherwise, the right to the money is lost.

The Eighth Amendment also forbids the government from imposing excessive fines. A fine is a sum of money that is to be paid as punishment for violating the law. A fine is also something (for example, money or property) that is paid or given up as punishment in a civil case to someone whose legally protected interests (such as rights, property, or well-being) have been harmed.

Finally, the Eighth Amendment forbids the government from imposing cruel and unusual punishments. The phrase "cruel and unusual punishments" refers to extremely harsh and painful punishments. The phrase also refers to punishments that are considered

"Let the punishment match the offense."

—*Marcus Tullius Cicero (106–43 B.C.), Roman political leader, lawyer, public speaker, and author*

to be much more serious than the offense. Although most Americans probably think of the cruel and unusual punishment clause in relation to the death penalty, the U.S. Supreme Court has also considered whether the amendment applies to cases involving lesser forms of physical punishments, for example, the physical punishment (called "corporal punishment") of schoolchildren by school

This photograph shows prisoners being punished in a prison in Delaware during the early 20th century. The two prisoners above are in pillories. The prisoner below is being whipped while tied to a whipping post. (*Library of Congress, Prints and Photographs Division, George Grantham Bain Collection [LC-USZ62-98905]*)

officials. In *Ingraham v. Wright* (1977), the Court said that the cruel and unusual punishments clause applies only to those convicted and imprisoned for crimes; therefore, corporal punishment was not cruel and unusual punishment. In *Youngberg v. Romero* (1982), the Court said that the cruel and unusual punishments clause does not apply to cases involving people who are put under the care and control of institutions for reasons other than punishment, for example, people who are placed in mental institutions.

ORIGINS

The history of the Eighth Amendment begins with the history of the English right to bail. The right to bail can be traced to the Statute of Westminster I of 1275. The statute listed in detail offenses that were bailable and those that were not. The statute, one of three declared by King Edward I in the English Parliament at Westminster, England, was practically a code of law that covered a wide range of legal issues. The statute also included much unwritten law. For five-and-a-half centuries, Westminster I was the basic source on the subject of which offenses did or did not require bail.

The Petition of Right of 1628, which declared the right not to be imprisoned without a good legal reason, was a response to an English case concerning bail. Darnel's case involved the case of five knights who were imprisoned for refusing to pay money to King Charles I.

Needing money to pay for England's wars with Spain and France, King Charles I imposed a forced loan. Forced loans were sums of money, disguised as loans, that some English monarchs forced subjects to pay. Although called "loans," monarchs who imposed forced loans never repaid them. The judges declared the forced loan imposed by Charles illegal. In response, Charles dismissed the chief justice and ordered that more than 70 knights and gentlemen be arrested for refusing to contribute to the loan.

In March 1627, Sir Thomas Darnel and four other knights were arrested for refusing to pay the loan. The knights demanded that the Crown explain in court why they should be in prison, or let them be freed on bail. In Darnel's case (1627), also called the Five Knights' case, the judges refused to release the knights on bail, but the judges did not say that the Crown could always imprison subjects without reason. The knights were freed in 1628.

Darnel's case helped move the English Parliament to pass the Petition of Right in 1628. The Petition of Right is a statement of complaints against Charles I and a statement of rights that Parliament wanted the king to recognize. Although Charles tried not to approve the petition, he was forced to do so. The petition declares, among other rights, the right of subjects not to be imprisoned without a good legal reason being shown.

Fifty years after Darnel's case, Crown officers undermined the right to bail again by using legal tricks to undermine the nearly century-old right to the writ of habeas corpus. A writ of habeas corpus is a legal order that a prisoner be brought before the court so that it can decide whether the prisoner has been lawfully imprisoned. *Habeas corpus* also refers to the right of a prisoner to get a writ of habeas corpus in order to protect against being illegally imprisoned. Habeas corpus, which is the opening phrase of the writ, is an order to jailers to bring the prisoner before the court. (The Latin phrase "habeas corpus" means "you should have the body.") To defend the right to the writ of habeas corpus, Parliament passed the Habeas Corpus Act in 1679. The act created procedures for gaining release from prison and included penalties for judges who violated the act. The U.S. Constitution, in Article 1, Section 9, also protects the right of habeas corpus, "unless when in cases of rebellion or invasion the public safety may require" that the right be suspended.

After Parliament passed the Habeas Corpus Act in 1679, judges defeated the act's intent by setting bail above what prisoners could pay. In response, Parliament inserted this clause in the English Bill of Rights of 1689: "That excessive bail ought not to be required, nor excessive fines imposed, nor cruel and unusual punishments inflicted." The ban against cruel and unusual punishments was meant to restrict tortures and extremely cruel punishments that were commonly used in England at the time. The Eighth Amendment restates the clause in the English Bill of Rights practically word for word.

THE RIGHT AGAINST EXCESSIVE BAIL

Bail is meant to solve the problem of what to do with the accused between arrest and trial: Releasing the accused from prison until trial makes their escape possible. On the other hand, keeping the accused in prison punishes people who may never be found guilty, makes preparing for their defense harder, and may make jurors more likely to believe that defendants are guilty. Thus, bail supports the principle that the accused are legally assumed to be innocent while reducing the risk that they will try to escape.

The Eighth Amendment, however, does not guarantee the right to be freed before trial: The amendment guarantees only the right against unreasonably high bail. Also, whether James Madison or Congress intended the Eighth Amendment to imply a right to bail is at most unclear. On the other hand, the bail clause has been read as implying a right to have the court set the amount of bail required, since otherwise, the clause would not be very important.

Courts usually grant bail for those arrested for civil offenses. Courts can use more judgment in the case of those arrested for crimes. The more serious the crime, the more likely a court will deny bail. For example, courts usually deny bail for those arrested for killing someone else.

CAPITAL PUNISHMENT

The Eighth Amendment is at the center of the hotly debated issue of capital punishment (death as punishment for a crime). Those who oppose the death penalty argue that it violates the amendment's ban against cruel and unusual punishments. Opponents also argue that the death penalty is not applied fairly: Certain groups of people convicted of crimes, especially African Americans and the poor, are more likely to receive the death penalty. Those who support capital punishment point out that it was an accepted practice in early America. In fact, when the Eighth Amendment was adopted, every state in the United States permitted execution (putting someone to death) for certain crimes. Also, the Fifth Amendment says that no person "shall be deprived of life . . . without due process of law." This would imply that the Constitution does not forbid capital punishment.

History of Executions in England and America

Many crimes were punishable by death in England during the 17th and 18th centuries. Executions were also public, and in the 18th

> "The death penalty has been [used] throughout our history, and, in a day when it is still widely accepted, it cannot be said to violate the [Eighth Amendment]."
>
> —*Chief Justice Earl Warren, delivering the opinion of the U.S. Supreme Court in* Trop v. Dulles *(1958)*

This 1951 photograph shows Julius and Ethel Rosenberg leaving the U.S. Court House after being found guilty of giving secret military information to the Soviet Union. They were sentenced to death the same year and executed on June 19, 1953. The Rosenbergs were the first U.S. civilians to be executed for spying. *(Library of Congress, Prints and Photographs Division [LC-USZ62-117772])*

century, large crowds went to see them. The crowds also often became unruly and violent afterward. By the end of the 18th century, 200 crimes were capital crimes. Despite this, many of those who committed capital crimes escaped the death penalty. Juries or courts were often unwilling to convict those charged with capital crimes. Many others received a reprieve (a delay of the death sentence) or a royal pardon. To receive a pardon or a reprieve, capital offenders usually had to agree to be sent to the American colonies. After the American Revolution, capital offenders were sent to Australia.

By the 17th century, capital offenders who could prove that they could read also escaped the death penalty. To escape death, a capital offender usually only had to read (or repeat from memory) the first verse of Psalm 51 of the Bible: "Have mercy on me, O God, according to your steadfast love; according to your abundant mercy blot out my transgressions [sins]." Psalm 51 came to be known as the "neck verse" (because it had the power to save someone's neck).

By the 19th century, only four crimes in England were capital crimes: murder, treason, arson (the illegal setting of property on fire) in a royal dockyard, and piracy (robbery on the open sea or ocean) with violence. Also, the public turned against public executions, and England banned them in 1868. In 1965, England ended capital punishment for all murders. Instead, people convicted of murder are today sentenced to life in prison. In 1971, arson in a royal dockyard became a non-capital crime.

In the United States, although not as many crimes were punishable by death as they were in England, executions for murderers and rapists were common in the United States until the 1960s. The number of executions was highest during the Great Depression (a period of great economic decline in the United States and other parts of the world from 1929 to about 1939). During this period, the federal government and the states executed, in total, between 150 and 200 people each year. The number fell to about 50 per year by the late 1950s (see graph, "People Executed, 1930–2003"). Parts of the United States continued to hold public executions until the 1930s.

BENEFIT OF CLERGY

The custom of allowing capital offenders who could read to escape the death penalty developed from something called the benefit of clergy. A member of the clergy (also called a cleric) is a religious official. In the Middle Ages, only church courts could try or sentence priests accused of crimes. In the late 12th century, church officials forced King Henry II of England and the royal courts to give the same privilege to clerks (Catholic clerics who were below priests) accused of capital crimes. Being able to read was the only proof that one was approved to be a priest.

Clerks who received benefit of clergy were turned over to the local bishop to be tried in the bishop's court. The court never sentenced convicted clerks to death and often acquitted them. Later, capital offenders who could show even the weakest connection to the church could also claim benefit of clergy. Although capital offenders who received benefit of clergy could be set free, judges had the power to sentence these offenders to prison for up to a year. Church courts rarely sentenced capital offenders to death; in cases where capital punishment was imposed, local nonchurch officials carried out the death sentences. In the 14th century, royal judges allowed laymen (men who were not clerics) convicted of capital crimes to receive benefit of clergy if they could show that they could read. Women were allowed to claim benefit of clergy in 1629.

Capital offenders were allowed to claim benefit of clergy only once. To make sure that criminals would not claim benefit of clergy again, they were branded on the thumb with an "M" (for murder) or a "T" (for theft). Branding was stopped in 1779. Benefit of clergy ended in England in 1827.

In the American colonies, most judges allowed capital offenders to claim benefit of clergy. In 1790, the United States ended benefit of clergy for all federal crimes. By the mid-19th century, no state court in the United States granted benefit of clergy.

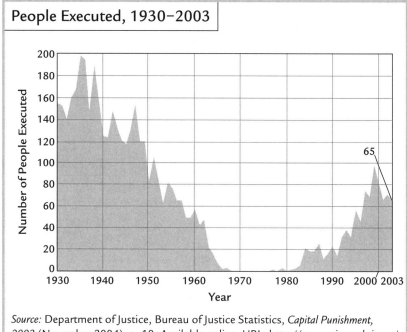

People Executed, 1930–2003

Source: Department of Justice, Bureau of Justice Statistics, *Capital Punishment, 2003* (November 2004), p. 10. Available online. URL: http://www.ojp.usdoj.gov/bjs/abstract/cp03.htm. Downloaded on November 21, 2004.

This graph shows the number of people executed in the United States from 1930 to 2003. The number of executions was highest during the Great Depression (which lasted from 1929 to about 1939). During this period, between 150 and 200 people were executed in the United States each year.

THE CAPITAL PUNISHMENT CASES OF 1972 AND 1976

In *Furman v. Georgia* (1972), the U.S. Supreme Court said that capital punishment as then practiced was unconstitutional because the death penalty was imposed randomly and unfairly. *Furman* involved the case of William Henry Furman. At 2 A.M. on August 11, 1967, in Savannah, Georgia, Furman, an African-American man, was trying to break into the home of William J. Micke, Jr., to rob it. Awakened by a noise, Micke came downstairs to investigate it. Micke was a white Coast Guard petty officer, a husband, and the father of five children. Furman ran to the back porch, tripped over an electrical cord, and fell. The gun that he was carrying accidentally fired, killing Micke through the closed kitchen door of the house. Furman was quickly caught. He was later convicted of murder and sentenced to death.

Furman was decided along with two other death penalty cases. One case involved an African-American man convicted of rape; the other case involved an African-American man convicted of murder. By the time of the *Furman* decision, critics of the death penalty had offered evidence that blacks received the death penalty more often than whites, and that people who had been convicted of crimes against whites received the death penalty much more often than those who had been convicted of crimes against blacks. In *Furman* and the other two cases decided along with it, the offenders were black and the victims were white. Each of the nine justices of the Court wrote a separate opinion. By a vote of 5 to 4, the Court reversed the death sentences in all three cases. Most of the justices agreeing with the Court opinion believed that the death penalty process in these cases showed a bias against black defendants. Associate Justices Thurgood Marshall and William J. Brennan, Jr., however, also believed that the death penalty was unconstitutional in all cases.

Furman canceled the death penalty in the United States. The Court, however, stopped short of saying that the Eighth Amendment absolutely outlawed capital punishment. Instead, the Court challenged the U.S. Congress and the state legislatures to develop new statutes to ensure that the death penalty would be applied fairly.

Immediately after *Furman,* at least 35 state legislatures began changing their death penalty laws. The new laws provided guidelines to help judges and juries determine when the death penalty should be used. A few states reacted to *Furman* by requiring the death penalty in certain cases, thereby taking the decision out of the hands of judges and juries.

Warren E. Burger, chief justice of the U.S. Supreme Court from 1969 to 1986, delivered the decision in *Furman v. Georgia* (1972), which said that capital punishment, as then practiced, was unconstitutional because the death penalty was imposed unfairly. *(Library of Congress, Prints and Photographs Division [LC-USZ62-60136])*

Potter Stewart, associate justice of the U.S. Supreme Court from 1958 to 1981, delivered the decision in *Gregg v. Georgia* (1976), which allowed certain states to bring back the death penalty. *(Library of Congress, Prints and Photographs Division [LC-USZ62-60143])*

In *Gregg v. Georgia* (1976), the Court allowed certain states to bring back capital punishment. *Gregg* involved the case of Troy Leon Gregg. On November 21, 1973, Fred Simmons and Bob Moore picked up Gregg and a teenage traveling companion, Floyd Allen, who were hitchhiking on the Florida Turnpike. While driving north, the car broke down. Using cash, Simmons bought a used car to replace the broken-down car. Later, they picked up another hitchhiker, Dennis Weaver. The other men dropped off Weaver in Atlanta at about 11 P.M. A short time later, the men stopped along the road in Gwinnett County for a break. Simmons and Moore left the car. Allen later told officers that Gregg then said that he intended to rob Simmons and Moore. Laying in wait for Simmons and Moore, Gregg shot them as they walked back toward the car. After being shot, Simmons and Moore fell near a ditch. Gregg then went up to Simmons and Moore and shot each of them in the head. Gregg then robbed them and drove away with Allen.

After reading about the shootings in an Atlanta newspaper, Weaver contacted the Gwinnett County police and told them about his journey with the victims and described Simmons's car. The next afternoon, officers

> "These death sentences are cruel and unusual in the same way that being struck by lightning is cruel and unusual [because they were imposed by chance]."
>
> —*Potter Stewart, associate justice of the U.S. Supreme Court, delivering his concurring opinion in* Furman v. Georgia *(1972)*

THE ELECTRIC CHAIR

Before the use of lethal injection, most condemned prisoners in the United States were executed in the electric chair. In this method of execution, the prisoner is strapped into a wired chair. Electrodes are then fastened to the prisoner's head and to the calf of one of the prisoner's legs. An electrical shock is then sent through the prisoner's body. If necessary, several shocks are applied.

The electric chair was first used in New York at Auburn State Prison on August 6, 1890. Pennsylvania adopted the electric chair in 1915. In time, 24 states adopted the electric chair.

found Gregg and Allen in Simmons's car in Asheville, North Carolina, and arrested them. A Georgia jury convicted Gregg of armed robbery and murder and sentenced him to death.

In 1976, the Court decided *Gregg* along with four other cases. In these five cases, the Court had to decide whether the death penalty violated the Eighth Amendment, and whether the revised death penalty statutes of Georgia, Texas, Florida, North Carolina, and Louisiana were constitutional. In *Gregg,* the Court said that the Georgia death penalty was constitutional. The Court also upheld the death penalty statutes of Texas and Florida, but declared that the statutes of North Carolina and Louisiana were illegal. The Court rejected the death penalty laws of North Carolina and Louisiana because they made the death penalty automatic for certain crimes.

In July 1980, Gregg and three other prisoners sentenced to death escaped. They were the first prisoners to escape Georgia's

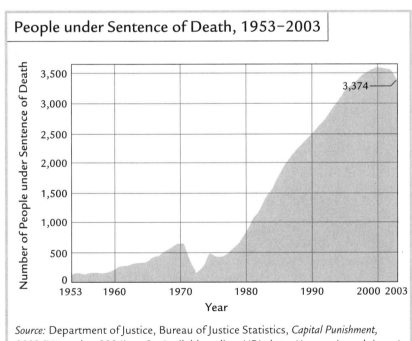

People under Sentence of Death, 1953–2003

Source: Department of Justice, Bureau of Justice Statistics, *Capital Punishment, 2003* (November 2004), p. 3. Available online. URL: http://www.ojp.usdoj.gov/bjs/abstract/cp03.htm. Downloaded on March 4, 2004.

The number of people sentenced to death began to rise in 1977, the year following the U.S. Supreme Court's decision in *Gregg v. Georgia* (1976). The number of prisoners on death row rose dramatically between 1980 and 2003.

death row (the prison area that houses prisoners sentenced to death). Their freedom, however, was brief. Gregg was beaten to death later that night in a bar in North Carolina. The other convicts were captured three days later.

After *Gregg*, the number of people sentenced to death in the United States began to rise. Today, 38 of the 50 American states allow capital punishment. Although three-fourths of the states and the federal government allow the death penalty, from 1977 to 2003, two-thirds of all executions in the United States occurred in only five states—Florida, Missouri, Oklahoma, Texas, and Virginia. Texas had the most executions. Texas also had the most executions in 2003. From 1977 to 2004, 944 people were executed in the United States.

NUMBER OF EXECUTIONS, 1977–2004

Year	Number of Executions	Year	Number of Executions
1977	1	1991	14
1978	0	1992	31
1979	2	1993	38
1980	0	1994	31
1981	1	1995	56
1982	2	1996	45
1983	5	1997	74
1984	21	1998	68
1985	18	1999	98
1986	18	2000	85
1987	25	2001	66
1988	11	2002	71
1989	16	2003	65
1990	23	2004	59

Source: Capital Punishment Statistics, Department of Justice, Bureau of Justice Statistics. Available online. URL: http://www.ojp.usdoj.gov/bjs/cp.htm. Updated on January 13, 2005.

In the 1980s and 1990s, many decisions of the Court removed some of the roadblocks to executions. For example, in *Lockhart v. McCree* (1986), the Court said that people opposed to executions can be barred from serving as jurors in murder cases. In *Penry v. Lynaugh* (1989), the Court said that people who are mentally retarded can receive the death penalty. In *Stanford v. Kentucky* (1989), the Court said that teenagers who are at least 16 years old can receive the death penalty. Also, Court decisions in the 1990s reduced the appeals that death row prisoners could make to the federal courts. From 1986 to 2003, the number of prisoners on death row increased from 1,800 to 3,374. From 1991 to 2004, 801 people had been executed.

In the late 1990s, however, some U.S. states began to consider suspending the death penalty after a series of cases in which death row prisoners were found innocent because of new evidence. In some cases, advances in DNA testing had made the discovery of new evidence possible. In all living things, DNA is that part of the cell containing the information about how a living thing will look or act. Since the DNA code in each person (except for identical twins) is unique, scientists can use DNA obtained from body fluids, such as blood, to identify someone.

EXECUTIONS DURING 2003

State	Number of Executions	State	Number of Executions
Texas	24	Georgia	3
Oklahoma	14	Indiana	2
North Carolina	7	Missouri	2
Ohio	3	Virginia	2
Alabama	3	Federal	1
Florida	3	Arkansas	1
		Total	65

Source: Capital Punishment, 2003, Department of Justice, Bureau of Justice Statistics (November 2004), p. 1. Available online. URL: http://www.ojp.usdoj.gov/bjs/abstract/cp03.htm. Downloaded on November 21, 2004.

In 2000, concerned that the death penalty process in Illinois was unfair and "therefore immoral," Governor George Ryan suspended his state's death penalty. (In 2002, Maryland governor Parris Glendening became the only other state governor to suspend the death penalty.) Governor Ryan pointed out that, from 1977 to 2000, courts found that 13 of the state's death row prisoners had been wrongly convicted. He also noted that during that same period, Illinois had executed 12 people. On January 11, 2003, two

John Paul Stevens, associate justice of the U.S. Supreme Court since 1975, delivered the decision in *Atkins v. Virginia* (2002), which said that executing the mentally retarded violated the Eighth Amendment ban against cruel and unusual punishments. *(Library of Congress, Prints and Photographs Division [LC-USZ62-60142])*

> "For God's sake, if you acknowledge that you should not put children to death, acknowledge that you should not put to death the mentally retarded."
>
> —*Democrat Joseph R. Biden, Jr., senator from Delaware, during a debate in the Senate of the U.S. Congress, May 25, 1990*

days before he left office, the governor cleared Illinois's death row by pardoning four prisoners, reducing the sentences of 164 others to life in prison, and reducing the sentences of three prisoners to 40 years to life. On January 20, 2004, Illinois adopted a new law designed to reduce the risk of executing innocent people. For example, the law forbids the state from executing the mentally retarded, allows the state supreme court to overturn a death sentence if the court finds the sentence to be "fundamentally unjust," and allows DNA testing for all criminal cases.

Also, in *Atkins v. Virginia* (2002), the Court reversed itself and said that executing the mentally retarded violated the Eighth Amendment. In *Ring v. Arizona* (2002), the Court said that only a jury, not a judge, can sentence a convicted person to death. After rising steadily during the 1980s and 1990s, the number of U.S. prisoners on death row decreased each year from 2001 to 2003. In 2001, the number of prisoners on death row decreased from 3,601 in 2000 to 3,577. In 2002, the number decreased to 3,562. The number of people executed also decreased in 2003, from 71 in 2002 to 65, the lowest number since 1996. In 2005, the Court said in *Roper v. Simmons* that the Eighth and Fourteenth Amendments bar executing people who were under 18 years old when they committed their crimes.

METHODS OF EXECUTION IN THE UNITED STATES

In 1982, Texas became the first state to execute a prisoner by lethal injection. In this method of execution, after the prisoner has been strapped to a table or a wheeled, narrow bed, a deadly drug is forced into the prisoner's vein through a tube, which is inserted into the vein by a needle. Sometimes, the drug is delivered into two tubes, one in each arm. Today, most executions in the United States are by lethal injection. From 1977 to 2003, 81 percent of the 885 executions in the United States were by lethal injection (see table). In 2003, all but one of the 65 executions in the United States were by lethal injection. (The other execution was by electrocution.)

EXECUTIONS IN THE UNITED STATES, BY STATE AND METHOD, 1977–2003

State	Number Executed	Lethal Injection	Electro- cution	Lethal Gas	Hanging	Firing Squad
Federal system	3	3	0	0	0	0
Alabama	28	4	24	0	0	0
Arizona	22	20	0	2	0	0
Arkansas	25	24	1	0	0	0
California	10	8	0	2	0	0
Colorado	1	1	0	0	0	0
Delaware	13	12	0	0	1	0
Florida	57	13	44	0	0	0
Georgia	34	11	23	0	0	0
Idaho	1	1	0	0	0	0
Illinois	12	12	0	0	0	0
Indiana	11	8	3	0	0	0
Kentucky	2	1	1	0	0	0
Louisiana	27	7	20	0	0	0
Maryland	3	3	0	0	0	0
Mississippi	6	2	0	4	0	0
Missouri	61	61	0	0	0	0
Montana	2	2	0	0	0	0
Nebraska	3	0	3	0	0	0
Nevada	9	8	0	1	0	0
New Mexico	1	1	0	0	0	0
North Carolina	30	28	0	2	0	0
Ohio	8	8	0	0	0	0
Oklahoma	69	69	0	0	0	0
Oregon	2	2	0	0	0	0
Pennsylvania	3	3	0	0	0	0
South Carolina	28	23	5	0	0	0

(continues)

EXECUTIONS IN THE UNITED STATES, BY STATE AND METHOD, 1977–2003 *(continued)*

State	Number Executed	Lethal Injection	Electro-cution	Lethal Gas	Hanging	Firing Squad
Tennessee	1	1	0	0	0	0
Texas	313	313	0	0	0	0
Utah	6	4	0	0	0	2
Virginia	89	62	27	0	0	0
Washington	4	2	0	0	2	0
Wyoming	1	1	0	0	0	0
Total	885	718	151	11	3	2

Note: Thirty-two states and the federal government executed prisoners during this period.
Source: Department of Justice, Bureau of Justice Statistics, *Capital Punishment, 2003.* (November 2004), p. 17. Available online. URL: http://www.ojp.usdoj.gov/bjs/abstract/cp03.htm. Downloaded on November 21, 2004.

Before lethal injection became common, condemned prisoners in the United States most often faced electrocution (execution by electricity). In this method of execution, the condemned is electro-

METHODS OF EXECUTION

Before the 20th century, many societies carried out capital punishment in ways that were extremely cruel. In Ancient Rome, condemned murderers and traitors (those guilty of treason) were thrown from a cliff known as the Tarpeian Rock; those convicted of killing a parent were put in a sealed bag with a dog, a rooster, an ape, and a poisonous snake and drowned; some had to participate in a fight to the death; and some were crucified (had their wrists or hands and feet nailed or tied to a cross). In ancient China, the condemned could be sawed in half, skinned alive, or boiled. In Europe, the condemned could be boiled in oil, burned alive, beheaded, hanged, or drowned. In these and other societies throughout the world, the condemned have also been crushed, torn apart, stoned, and punished in other horrifying ways. Many of these forms of punishment are now considered extremely cruel and are outlawed almost everywhere. By the end of the 20th century, many governments around the world, including almost every state in the United States, had begun executing the condemned by lethal injection.

cuted by means of a special chair called an electric chair. Some states still allow the use of the electric chair. Other methods of execution still approved for use in the United States include the gas chamber (poisoning the condemned in a small sealed chamber with gas), the firing squad (a small group of people who shoot the condemned to death), and hanging. See the table (pages 75–76) for more on execution methods.

As of December 31, 2003, 37 states allowed the use of lethal injection as a method of execution. Also, 14 states allowed the condemned to choose between lethal injection and one other method; five of these states, however, allowed this only if the condemned was sentenced to death before a particular date. Three states allowed the use of another method of execution besides lethal injection only if it had been declared unconstitutional. The federal government executes prisoners by lethal injection.

6

Legal Rights and the War on Terrorism

On September 11, 2001, the United States suffered a series of horrific terrorist attacks resulting in more than 3,000 deaths. After the attacks, the United States declared war against terrorism. The United States vowed to bring its full might against those responsible for the terrorist attacks and against any others suspected of plotting future attacks. The executive branch also worked to expand its power in order to prevent another "September 11." This expansion of government power greatly affected rights guaranteed under the Fourth through Eighth Amendments.

THE TERRORIST ATTACKS OF SEPTEMBER 11, 2001

At 8:46 A.M. Eastern Daylight Time on September 11, 2001, American Airlines Flight 11 crashed into the 110-story north tower of the World Trade Center in New York City. Seventeen minutes later, as people on the ground and television viewers across the world watched the burning 110-story skyscraper, United Airlines Flight 175 crashed into the south tower of the trade center, causing a great explosion. Less than two hours after the first crash, both towers had collapsed.

The two crashes left no doubt: They were not accidents. At 9:20 A.M., the FBI announced that it was investigating reports that planes were being hijacked (taken control of by force). Ten minutes later, President Bush declared, "We have had a national tragedy. Two airplanes have crashed into the World Trade Center in an apparent terrorist attack on our country."

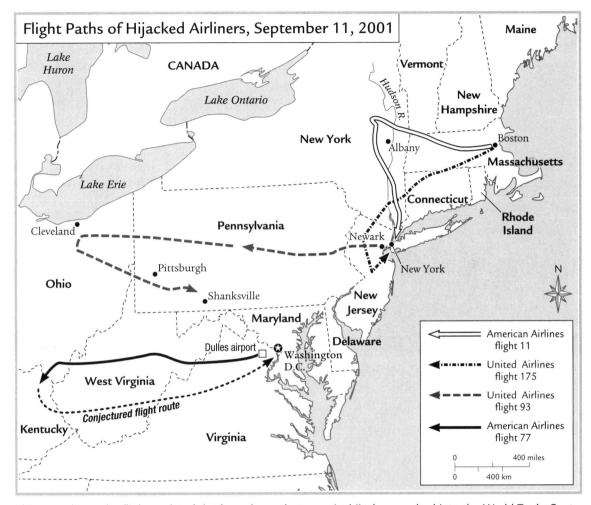

This map shows the flight paths of the four planes that terrorist hijackers crashed into the World Trade Center in New York City, into the Pentagon in Washington, D.C., and in Shanksville, Pennsylvania, on September 11, 2001.

The World Trade Center would not be the only target. At 9:40 A.M., American Airlines Flight 77 crashed into the Pentagon, the headquarters of the U.S. Department of Defense, in Washington, D.C. At 10:03 A.M., United Airlines Flight 93, probably heading for another target in Washington, D.C., crashed 80 miles southeast of Pittsburgh in a field near Shanksville, Pennsylvania. Before the crash, the plane's passengers, who had found out about the earlier crashes from callers to their cell phones, had tried to overpower the terrorists.

The burning Twin Towers after the terrorist attacks on the World Trade Center in New York City on September 11, 2001 *(Library of Congress, Prints and Photographs Division [LC-DIG-ppmsca-02137])*

The attacks on September 11 killed about 2,800 people in New York City, 184 at the Pentagon, and 45 in Pennsylvania. Among those killed were the 19 hijackers; the 266 airline passengers and crew in the hijacked planes; and several hundred police officers, firefighters, and other emergency workers, who were crushed when the towers collapsed.

Nineteen hijackers carried out the suicide attacks. All of the hijackers were from the Middle East (the group of countries in southwest Asia and North Africa). Fifteen hijackers were from Saudi Arabia (in southwest Asia). The hijackers were connected with al-Qaeda, a terrorist group founded in the late 1980s by Osama bin Laden, a member of one of Saudi Arabia's wealthiest families.

Members of al-Qaeda are followers of Islam. Muhammed, an Arab born in Mecca, in what is now called Saudi Arabia, founded the religion of Islam in the seventh century. Muslims, followers of Islam, believe that Allah is the only God and that Muhammed was his prophet. They also believe in the Koran, a book of sacred writings that followers believe Allah revealed to Muhammed.

Al-Qaeda opposes Islamic governments that it views as corrupt and the presence of the United States in Islamic lands. Before

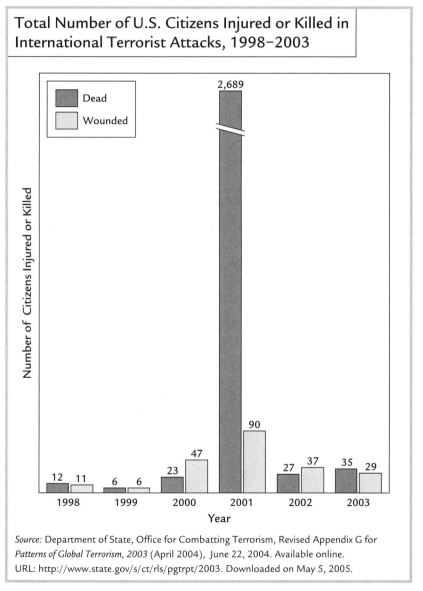

Total Number of U.S. Citizens Injured or Killed in International Terrorist Attacks, 1998–2003

Source: Department of State, Office for Combatting Terrorism, Revised Appendix G for *Patterns of Global Terrorism, 2003* (April 2004), June 22, 2004. Available online. URL: http://www.state.gov/s/ct/rls/pgtrpt/2003. Downloaded on May 5, 2005.

This graph shows the number of U.S. citizens killed by terrorist attacks from 1998 to 2003.

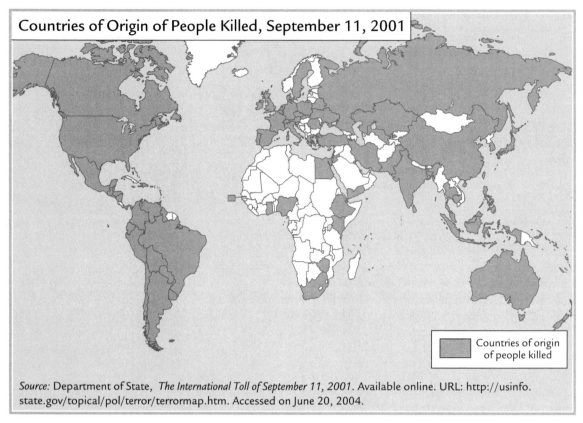

Countries of Origin of People Killed, September 11, 2001

Countries of origin
of people killed

Source: Department of State, *The International Toll of September 11, 2001*. Available online. URL: http://usinfo. state.gov/topical/pol/terror/terrormap.htm. Accessed on June 20, 2004.

This map shows the countries of origin of people killed in the terrorist attacks of September 11, 2001.

September 11, al-Qaeda had already carried out many terrorist attacks, including the bombing of U.S. embassies (the official homes and offices of U.S. ambassadors) in the African countries of Kenya and Tanzania, and the bombing of the U.S. warship *Cole* in the Arab country of Yemen.

THE WAR AGAINST AFGHANISTAN

Al-Qaeda was based in Afghanistan, a Middle Eastern country in western Asia. The Taliban, a religious and political group that controlled most of Afghanistan, had made the country a haven for al-Qaeda and other Islamic militant groups. A week after the attacks, the United States warned the Taliban forces to hand over Osama bin Laden. The Taliban refused. On October 7, 2001, the United States and Britain began a war against al-Qaeda and Taliban forces

Afghanistan under the Taliban, 2001

The Taliban had made Afghanistan a haven for al-Qaeda, the terrorist group that planned the attacks against the United States on September 11, 2001. On October 7, the United States and Great Britain began a war against Afghanistan by launching air strikes against targets in the country. In December, the United States and military allies drove the Taliban from power.

by launching air strikes against targets in Afghanistan. In December, the United States and military allies drove the Taliban from power. During the war in Afghanistan, the United States captured or killed thousands of Islamic militants. Those who remained went into hiding.

LEGAL RIGHTS
AFTER SEPTEMBER 11, 2001

After the terrorist attacks of September 11, 2001, the U.S. Congress expanded the federal government's power to search and seize, to hold suspects and witnesses, and to bring suspects to trial. Congress also limited the legal rights of people suspected of being terrorists or of helping them. Moreover, U.S. president George W. Bush defined the attacks not as criminal acts, but as acts of war, and declared terrorists to be enemy fighters in a war against the United States. The Bush administration (the executive branch under President Bush) claimed that people suspected of being terrorists, or "enemy combatants," did not have the right of habeas corpus, the right to a lawyer, or other rights that suspects usually have under the U.S. Constitution.

Thus, the government's reaction to the terrorist attacks affected the rights of citizens and noncitizens. Unlike certain other parts of the U.S. Constitution (for example, Article 2, Section 1, which requires that the president of the United States be a citizen), the Bill of Rights mentions "people" and "persons," but not citizens. This suggests that the Bill of Rights also protects immigrants (foreign-born noncitizens living in the United States) and other noncitizens.

Spying

On May 30, 2002, U.S. attorney general John Ashcroft (the nation's chief law officer) increased the power of the FBI to spy on Americans in public places or at public events in order to prevent or find out about terrorism and other crimes. Among legal observers, this called into question whether federal agents are actually conducting a "search" under the Fourth Amendment when they, for example, spy on people walking in a protest march, attending a political rally, visiting an open Internet chat room, or attending a public religious service. On the one hand, such "spying" would seem not to violate anyone's privacy. On the other hand, someone who is constantly being watched, either by the government or a private person, may feel that his or her privacy is being invaded. Also, people who believe that the government is watching them may be less willing to express their views or even to attend certain events.

Moreover, many legal observers are also concerned about high-tech spying (spying with scientifically advanced devices). Such spying has become much more advanced since the U.S. Supreme Court addressed government wiretapping in *Katz v. United States* in 1967. For example, wireless microphones can pick up a conversation hundreds of feet away; a GPS (global positioning system), which

"We are rapidly entering the age of no privacy, where everyone is open to surveillance at all times; where there are no secrets from government."

—*William O. Douglas, associate justice of the U.S. Supreme Court, delivering his dissenting opinion in* Osborn v. United States *(1966)*

TERRORISM INFORMATION AWARENESS

In 2002, the Defense Advanced Research Projects Agency (a branch of the U.S. Department of Defense) announced Total Information Awareness (TIA), the agency's project to develop a massive computer system that would search through many public and private computer databases (collections of information stored in computers) to spot signs of terrorist plots and to identify and track terrorists. The system would search personal information, such as credit card, medical, school, and travel records. Using a computer to search through one or more computer databases to uncover relationships and patterns is called data mining.

TIA provoked strong criticisms by privacy rights supporters, lawmakers, and others who feared that TIA would threaten privacy. The Defense Department tried to assure U.S. lawmakers that TIA would have safeguards to protect privacy. The department also renamed the project Terrorism Information Awareness in May 2003. Nevertheless, on September 25, 2003, the U.S. Congress stopped providing money for TIA. Congress, however, continued to provide money for programs to use data mining for gathering foreign intelligence.

TIA was not the only government data-mining program. The federal government is using or developing many systems that use data mining to spot terrorists or to prevent terrorism. For example, on August 26, 2004, the Transportation Security Administration (TSA), an agency in the Department of Homeland Security, announced that it would begin testing Secure Flight, a new system to prescreen airline passengers, by the end of the year. Prescreening involves separating passengers into those who need to be checked more carefully and those who do not. Secure Flight will check the identities of U.S. travelers by comparing information supplied by the airlines about passengers against information in government databases. The system is designed to target more accurately passengers who should be screened more carefully.

Secure Flight replaces another proposed system known as CAPPS II (Computer-Assisted Passenger Prescreening System II). This system would have used information from private and government databases to verify a passenger's personal information —full name, home address, home phone number, and date of birth—and to decide whether a passenger was "no risk," "unknown risk," or "high risk." Critics had complained that CAPPS II did not have enough safeguards to protect privacy. According to the TSA, unlike CAPPS II, Secure Flight will seek to identify only known or suspected terrorists.

uses the signals of a satellite (an object put into space to circle the earth) to track people or objects, can show where someone or something is anytime or anywhere; the Internet can allow someone to secretly read someone else's private e-mails, to see which Web sites someone visits, and to see someone's personal medical or bank records; electronic devices called pen registers can record all the telephone numbers someone has called from a particular phone line. In the near future, companies could create a GPS that could be placed in humans.

In 2002, the police department in Washington, D.C., began expanding its electronic surveillance system. It is now one of the country's largest networks of spy cameras. From a command center, officers can watch images from video cameras installed across the city. The police installed 13 cameras near the White House, the Washington Monument, major bridges, and other landmarks, which the cameras scan automatically. The officers can also zoom in on people. Most of the cameras are hidden from public view or disguised. The network also links hundreds of government video cameras that were already watching government buildings, streets, subway stations, and other public areas. Images can also be beamed to computer screens in police squad cars. After the terrorist attacks of September 11, 2001, federal government officials began looking to video surveillance as a way to help protect national security.

In cases involving high-tech spying, the Court considers, as it did in *Katz*, whether the person being spied on has a reasonable expectation of privacy. For example, in *Smith v. Maryland* (1979), the Court said that the government's use of pen registers does not violate the Fourth Amendment because callers cannot reasonably expect that the numbers they call will be private. Another issue is whether such spying requires the government to have a warrant. For example, in *State v. Jackson* (2003), the Supreme Court of Washington said that the police need a warrant to use a GPS to track a suspect. As spying devices become smaller and better, they could allow the government to intrude even more into people's private affairs. Such devices will also become harder to notice or find, thereby making illegal spying harder to discover.

Enemy Combatants

On January 11, 2002, the United States began moving people captured during the war in Afghanistan to the U.S. naval base at Guantánamo Bay, Cuba (an island lying between the southeast part of North America and the north part of South America). The federal government believes that the prisoners, who were captured mainly in Afghanistan and the neighboring country of Pakistan, are members of the Taliban or of al-Qaeda. As of April 2004, more than 600 prisoners from more than 24 countries were at Guantánamo. By May 2004, the government had released 146 prisoners, 12 of whom were being held in their home countries. So far, the government has formally charged only a few of the prisoners with a crime. The government also seized U.S. citizens in Afghanistan who were connected with the Taliban. These citizens, however, were transferred to the United states after the war.

The Bush administration claimed that the prisoners at Guantánamo Bay are not prisoners of war, but unlawful combatants (fighters in a war). Under international law, prisoners of war (lawful combatants) have certain rights, such as the right against being tortured. The Bush administration argued that the members of al-Qaeda and the Taliban held at Guantánamo do not qualify as prisoners of war for several reasons. For example, al-Qaeda violates the rules of war by attacking civilians (people who are not soldiers). Also, neither members of the Taliban nor those of al-Qaeda wore uniforms, which enable soldiers to avoid targeting civilians.

The Bush administration also denied that the prisoners at Guantánamo had the right of habeas corpus. In wartime, the U.S. Congress has the power (under Article 1, Section 9 of the U.S. Constitution) to end the right to habeas corpus for a time, but Congress has not done so. Human rights groups and foreign governments criticized the Bush administration for not declaring the detainees to be prisoners of war and for denying them access to the courts and to lawyers.

In *Rasul v. Bush* (2004), the U.S. Supreme Court considered whether the prisoners at Guantánamo had the right of habeas corpus. Up to this point, except in a few cases, the federal courts had supported President Bush's view of the president's power and refused requests on behalf of prisoners to consider whether they were being held lawfully. Along with *Rasul,* the Court also heard *Al Odah v. United States* (2004). The family members of 16 former and current prisoners at Guantánamo Bay brought the cases. The 16 prisoners are citizens of Great Britain, Australia, and Kuwait (a country in southwest Asia). Shafiq Rasul and Fawzi Khalid Abdullah Fahad Al Odah, citizens of Great Britain and Australia, had already been released from Guantánamo Bay by the time the cases reached the Court.

On April 20, 2004, the federal government argued before the Court that the government had the power to hold non–U.S. citizens at Guantánamo for as long as the government believed was necessary. The government claimed that such power was necessary because the country is at war against terrorists, who, if released, would threaten the nation's security. The government also denied that the prisoners at Guantánamo had the right of habeas corpus. Since the U.S. naval base at Guantánamo Bay is still formally a part of Cuba, the government claimed that U.S. courts had no power to hear cases involving the prisoners. Critics, however, said that Cuba has supreme power over Guantánamo Bay in name only; in reality, the United States has total control over Guantánamo Bay.

In *Rasul*, decided on June 28, 2004, the Court said that it has the power to hear cases brought on behalf of foreign nationals at Guantánamo Bay challenging the lawfulness of their imprisonment. The Court also said that it had the power to hear the complaints of the prisoners involved in *Al Odah*.

The U.S. Supreme Court under William H. Rehnquist, associate justice of the Court from 1972 to 1986 and chief justice from 1986 to 2005, said in *Rasul v. Bush* (2004) that the foreign nationals held at Guantánamo Bay, Cuba, have the right to ask a court to consider whether the government is keeping them in prison lawfully. On the same day, the Court said in *Hamdi v. Rumsfeld* (2004) that citizens held in the United States by the government as enemy combatants also have this right. *(Library of Congress, Prints and Photographs Division [LC-USZ62-60141])*

Since September 11, 2001, the federal government has also held U.S. citizens as enemy combatants. The Bush administration claimed that U.S. courts have no power to review a decision by the military that a citizen is an enemy combatant. On April 28, 2004, in *Hamdi v. Rumsfeld* (2004) and *Rumsfeld v. Padilla* (2004), the federal government argued before the Court that the government has the right to hold citizens as enemy combatants without formally charging them with a crime. The government also argued that enemy combatants do not have the right to communicate with a lawyer.

Hamdi involved the case of Yaser Esam Hamdi. The Northern Alliance (an Afghan group opposed to the Taliban) captured Hamdi on the battlefield in Afghanistan in 2001 and turned him over to the U.S. military. The government claimed that Hamdi was fighting with the Taliban. Hamdi, a Saudi Arabian citizen who grew up in the Middle East, was born in Baton Rouge, Louisiana.

Rumsfeld v. Padilla involved the case of Jose Padilla, a former Chicago, Illinois, gang member whom the government seized at O'Hare International Airport in Chicago in 2002. According to the government, Padilla had plotted with members of al-Qaeda to build and set off a radioactive bomb in the United States. The federal government allowed neither Hamdi nor Padilla to see a lawyer for two years. In *Rumsfeld,* the question before the Court was whether the president has the power as commander in chief of the military to hold as enemy combatants citizens captured in the United States.

The Court decided *Hamdi* and *Rumsfeld* on the same day that it decided *Rasul.* In *Hamdi,* the Court said that the government has the power to hold U.S. citizens as enemy combatants without charging them or putting them on trial. On the other hand, the prisoners have the right to challenge their imprisonment in court. In *Rumsfeld,* the Court said that it did not decide whether the president has the power to hold Padilla because the lawsuit on his behalf was filed in the wrong district. Padilla has to file his lawsuit again. Thus, the Court left unanswered the question of whether the president has the power to hold as enemy combatants citizens captured in the United States.

On October 11, 2004, the U.S. government freed Hamdi on the conditions that he give up his U.S. citizenship, renounce terrorism, and live in Saudi Arabia for five years. Hamdi's agreement with the United States also bars him from traveling to Afghanistan, Iraq, Israel, Syria, the West Bank (territory occupied by Israel), and the Gaza Strip (a region adjoining Egypt and Israel). The agreement also requires that he not sue the U.S. government for holding him and that he notify officials in Saudi Arabia if he finds out about "any planned or executed acts of terrorism."

The federal government is also holding people suspected of being terrorists in secret locations. These people—at least three

"[The U.S. Supreme Court has] long since made clear that a state of war is not a blank check for the President when it comes to the rights of the Nation's citizens."

—*Associate Justice Sandra Day O'Connor, delivering the opinion of the U.S. Supreme Court in* Hamdi v. Rumsfeld *(2004)*

men, according to news reports—are believed to be high-level members of al-Qaeda.

Communications between Lawyers and Prisoners

On October 30, 2001, Attorney General Ashcroft approved a rule that allows federal officials to sit in on meetings between federal prisoners and their lawyers if the federal government reasonably suspects that the prisoners may use what they and their lawyers say or write (or communicate in some other way) to each other to help carry out terrorist acts. The attorney general was concerned that some prisoners may hire lawyers to help carry out terrorist plans by, for example, sending messages to other terrorists. The attorney general's order also applies to witnesses who are not suspects, but who are held by the government because their testimony is necessary to a trial.

Traditionally, lawyers and their clients (including those not suspected of committing or charged with crimes) have the right to keep their communications secret. In the U.S. Supreme Court's decision in *Upjohn Co. v. United States* (1981), Associate Justice William H. Rehnquist said, "The attorney-client privilege is the oldest of the privileges for confidential communications known to the common law. . . . The privilege recognizes that sound legal advice or [defense] depends upon the lawyer's being fully informed by the client." Senator Patrick Leahy, chairman of the Senate Judiciary Committee, sent a letter dated November 9, 2001, to Attorney General Ashcroft criticizing his new policy. Leahy argued that it "profoundly compromised" the "fundamental right" to a lawyer.

Treatment of Immigrants

Nearly a week after the terrorist attacks of September 11, 2001, an airline captain asked a Pakistani American to leave the plane because the crew felt unsafe with him onboard. During the weeks following the attacks, other airlines also removed passengers because members of the flight crew or other passengers were afraid to fly with Muslims or Arabs (or people who looked like them). On the night of September 12, someone fired 13 or 14 bullets at the

This photo shows an immigrant family on Ellis Island, New York, looking at the Statue of Liberty. Ellis Island was the major entry port for immigrants to the United States from 1892 to 1924. During that period, about 17 million immigrants passed through Ellis Island. *(Library of Congress, Prints and Photographs Division [LC-USZ62-50904])*

Islamic Center in Irving, Texas. On September 15, a man shot a male Indian gas-station owner in Mesa, Arizona, to death, believing (wrongly) that the victim (who was wearing a turban) was an Arab or a Muslim. The same day, a man killed a Pakistani at his grocery store near Dallas, Texas. According to the FBI, reported cases of crimes driven by hatred of Muslims rose from 28 in 2000 to 481 in 2001, an increase of 1,600 percent.

President Bush tried to assure Arabs and Muslims in America and around the world that the United States did not blame all Arabs or Muslims for the terrorist attacks of September 11. Less than a week after the attacks, President Bush visited the Islamic Center in Washington, D.C., where he appealed to Americans to "treat each other with respect" and criticized Americans who would "take out their anger" against Muslims. The following week, the president met with Muslim community leaders at the White House.

Nevertheless, the government did not ignore that the terrorists of September 11, 2001, immigrated to the United States from the Middle East. After the attacks, law enforcement officers used federal immigration laws to hold or arrest immigrants, mostly Arabs and Muslims, suspected of having ties to the attacks or to terrorism in general. Through the newly passed USA PATRIOT Act, the U.S. Congress gave the federal government the power to hold immigrants or other noncitizens for as long as it wished and without setting a date for their release if the attorney general determined that there were "reasonable grounds to believe" that those being held had been involved in terrorism or some other activity that endangered national security, if they were staying in the country illegally, and if their country refused to accept them.

According to a report, dated April 2003, by the inspector general of the U.S. Department of Justice, two months after the terrorist attacks, federal, state, and local law enforcement officers across the nation had held more than 1,200 citizens and immigrants during the government's investigation of the attacks. The government has not reported the exact number of those held. After questioning them, the government later released many without charging them with breaking any criminal or immigration laws.

The government, however, arrested and held many of those seized after the attacks for violating federal immigration laws by, for example, staying longer than legally permitted or by entering the country illegally. Three months after the attacks, the federal government had arrested 658 immigrants as part of its investigation of the terrorist attacks. By early August 2002, the federal government had arrested 738 immigrants suspected of at least possibly having ties to terrorism. Nearly all of the immigrants held or arrested as part of the government's investigation of the terrorist attacks were Muslim men from Arab or South Asian countries. The government also deported (removed from the country) many Arab and Muslim men for violating immigration laws.

The government held many immigrants for months. According to news reports, at least one immigrant (who was seized on the night of September 11, 2001) has, so far, been held for years, even though the FBI has officially concluded that he has no ties to

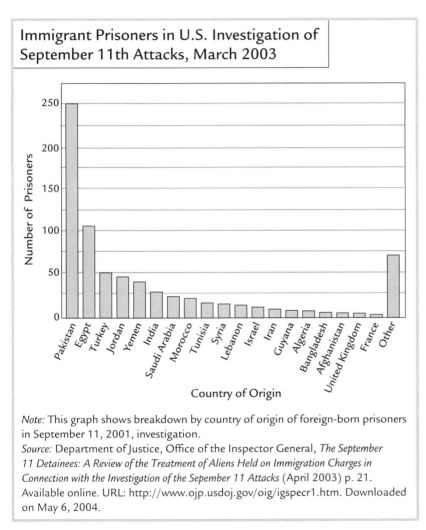

Immigrant Prisoners in U.S. Investigation of September 11th Attacks, March 2003

Note: This graph shows breakdown by country of origin of foreign-born prisoners in September 11, 2001, investigation.
Source: Department of Justice, Office of the Inspector General, *The September 11 Detainees: A Review of the Treatment of Aliens Held on Immigration Charges in Connection with the Investigation of the Sepember 11 Attacks* (April 2003) p. 21. Available online. URL: http://www.ojp.usdoj.gov/oig/igspecr1.htm. Downloaded on May 6, 2004.

Most of the immigrants held in the U.S. investigation are from Arab and Muslim countries.

terrorism. Prison officials also did not allow the prisoners to contact family, friends, or lawyers. The attorney general ordered that, for the sake of national security, deportation hearings (hearings to decide whether to deport an immigrant) that the federal government considers to be of "special interest" be closed to the public. Journalists, organizations, and family members of prisoners, however, uncovered and released information about individual prisoners.

Critics argue that the federal government's policy of holding certain people without saying when they can be released violates the prisoners' Fifth Amendment right to due process because holding people in this way gives them, in effect, a life sentence without clear proof that they have committed any crime.

The inspector general's report also found that, during the investigation of the terrorist attacks of September 11, 2001, the FBI did not carefully distinguish between immigrants suspected of having ties to terrorism and those immigrants who had no ties to terrorism. The report also found other problems: For example, it found that the federal government did not promptly tell immigrant prisoners of the charges against them, that prisons limited these prisoners' access to lawyers, and that prison officers had assaulted or harassed some of the prisoners.

Besides seizing people suspected of having ties to terrorism, on November 9, 2001, the FBI and other law enforcement officers began searching out and interviewing thousands of Arab, Muslim, and South Asian men from countries that the U.S. government had linked to terrorism. Besides questions relating to terrorism, law enforcement officers asked immigrants to provide personal information, such as where they worship, their religious practices, and the names and telephone numbers of friends and coworkers in the United States. The purpose of the interviews was to uncover terrorists. The government said that the interviews were voluntary. At least some immigrants, however, have said that they did not feel free to refuse to answer questions.

Finally, in June 2002, the federal government began tracking foreigners staying temporarily in the United States. Foreign visitors, such as students or workers, are foreigners permitted to stay in the United States for only a limited time. When a national (citizen or subject) of another country arrives to the United States, he or she must register with the federal government. The government scans fingerprints, takes digital photographs (pictures that can be stored in a computer), and questions those who register.

Until 2004, the tracking program required, with some exceptions, all young or adult men over the age of 15 who were nationals of 25 countries to register with the federal government. Except those from North Korea, all nationals required to register were from Arab or Muslim countries. The government held or deported thousands of men who registered for violating immigration laws. Some complained that the registration program unfairly treated all Arab and Muslim men as possible terrorists. In April 2004, the government began requiring all foreign visitors to register. The federal government also requires U.S. colleges and universities to report on their foreign students and to tell the government if they

BIOMETRICS

When foreign visitors enter the United States, immigration officials scan fingerprints and faces into a device that uses this information to check the identities of these visitors. Such devices use biometrics to identify people. *Biometrics* refers to ways of identifying people by measuring their unique features. All humans use a basic form of biometrics: A person recognizes a friend, for example, by the shape of the friend's face or the sound of his or her voice. Fingerprints and facial patterns are examples of what are called biometric identifiers. A person's iris (the colored part of the eye) and retina (the soft, thin layer of nerves lining the back of the eye) are also biometric identifiers. When someone scans a fingerprint into a biometric device to verify a person's identity, the device compares the fingerprint that has just been scanned with a sample of

the fingerprint that is stored in a computer database. Before the U.S. Congress ended funding for the Terrorism Information Awareness project, it had also planned to use biometric technology to identify and track terrorists.

Using facial patterns as biometric identifiers is called face recognition. Airports have tested face-recognition systems (or face scanners) designed to help spot terrorists. These systems search a database of images to find a match. In January 2001, the city of Tampa, Florida, used this type of face scanner at the National Football League's Super Bowl to scan faces in the crowds. So far, however, these systems have proven to be far less reliable than those used only to verify someone's identity, since these devices compare an image with only one image in the database.

violate school regulations. Critics charge that collecting personal information on foreign visitors threatens the privacy of people who may someday seek to live permanently in the United States, or who may someday become citizens.

7

The USA PATRIOT Act and the Future of American Legal Rights

Nearly two weeks after the terrorist attacks of September 11, 2001, Attorney General John Ashcroft sent the U.S. Congress a proposal asking it to give the president and the Department of Justice certain powers that, according to him, were necessary to prevent future terrorist attacks and to punish terrorists. On October 24, 2001, Congress responded by quickly passing the USA PATRIOT Act. The president signed the bill into law two days later.

The effect on U.S. law was sweeping: The PATRIOT Act made important changes to more than 15 important statutes. These changes greatly increased the power of the federal government to spy, investigate, and punish. The federal government now has much greater power to secretly watch, listen in on, and track communications (such as telephone calls, voice mail, and e-mail) in order to carry out the law and gather foreign intelligence, to control the actions of banks and other financial institutions in order to prevent terrorists from getting money to support acts of terrorism, to hold and deport immigrants suspected of being terrorists, and to prevent foreign terrorists from entering the country. Also, under the act, some crimes (such as terrorist attacks on buses, trains, or other forms of mass transportation) became federal crimes for the first time. The act also increased the punishment for many federal crimes and increased the statute of limitations for crimes of terrorism. (The statute of limitations for a crime is the legal deadline for charging someone with and punishing someone for the crime.) Several sections of the PATRIOT Act that relate to foreign intelligence and domestic spying will end on December 31, 2005, unless Congress renews these sections.

> "They that can give up essential liberty to obtain a little temporary safety deserve neither liberty nor safety."
>
> —*Benjamin Franklin (1706–90) in* Historical Review of Pennsylvania *(1759)*

BALANCING FREEDOM AND SECURITY

Throughout the ages, philosophers have argued that a country must balance freedom and security: The more free the society, the less safe and secure it is. For example, people who are free to speak their minds may also encourage others to commit acts of violence. A thief may remain free to steal again because police officers cannot arrest him/her without proof. On the other hand, a country whose government has the power to do whatever it wishes in the name of security is likely to have little or no freedom at all. Countries have defended putting people in prison for criticizing the government by arguing that such people promote

THE DEPARTMENT OF HOMELAND SECURITY

Nearly a month after the terrorist attacks of September 11, 2001, President George W. Bush created the White House Office of Homeland Security, whose task was to create a plan and direct the effort to protect the United States from future terrorist attacks. The president appointed Tom Ridge, then governor of Pennsylvania, to head the office.

Lawmakers called for turning the Office of Homeland Security into a new federal department so that it would have greater power. They also wanted to combine those areas of the government responsible for security into the new department. In June 2002, the Bush administration responded by proposing the Department of Homeland Security. On Friday, November 22, 2002, the U.S. Congress passed the Department of Homeland Security Act. The president signed the act into law the following Monday. The act created the new department out of the 22 agencies in the departments of Agriculture, Commerce, Defense, Energy, Health and Human Services, Justice, Transportation, and Treasury, and other independent bodies. On January 24, 2003, Ridge became secretary of the department. The agencies making up the new department began moving to the department in March 2003. The Department of Homeland Security represents the largest reorganization of the executive branch since the creation of the Department of Defense in 1947.

disorder or help foreign enemies by weakening support for the government.

Many Americans disagree over whether the USA PATRIOT Act achieves the right balance between freedom and security. Critics of the act argue that it threatens rights protected by the U.S. Constitution, including those protected by the Fourth, Fifth, Sixth, and Eighth Amendments. Specifically, critics complain that the act greatly increases the power of the federal government to obtain private information about individuals, eavesdrop on telephone conversations, look at private e-mails, keep track of Web site visits, and do other things. Moreover, critics complain, the act limits the power of judges to oversee or limit such actions. Critics also argue that the act allows the government to get around the Fourth Amendment by allowing the government to conduct certain searches without probable cause. Defenders of the USA PATRIOT Act argue that protecting the United States against terrorism requires Americans to give up some freedoms. Still, others believe that the USA PATRIOT Act does not give the federal government enough power to protect national security.

THE HOMELAND SECURITY ADVISORY SYSTEM

On March 12, 2002, Tom Ridge, head of the Office of Homeland Security, announced the Homeland Security Advisory System. The warning system uses five colors—green, blue, yellow, orange, and red—to notify the American public, federal agencies, and state and local governments about how likely terrorist attacks will happen in the United States. Each color represents a different level of risk. Red represents "severe" (the highest) risk, and green represents "low" (the lowest) risk. Blue (which represents a "guarded" risk) is higher than green; yellow (which represents an "elevated" risk) is higher than blue; and orange (which represents a "high" risk) is higher than yellow.

After consulting with members of the Homeland Security Advisory Council and the secretary of homeland security, the

(continues)

(continued)

attorney general announces the level of risk to the public and the proper federal, state, and local officials. The Homeland Security Advisory Council, which is made up of leaders from state and local governments, business, and academic institutions, and other leaders, advises the secretary of homeland security. Each threat level triggers specific responses by federal agencies and state and local governments. The federal government also advises the public to take certain actions depending on the level of risk. For example, depending on the level of risk, federal, state, and local agencies may watch certain areas, such as airports, ports, and government buildings, more closely; the federal government may advise the public to store food, water, and other supplies, and to report suspicious activities to government officials. When Secretary Ridge announced the advisory system, the United States was in the yellow condition. By late 2004, the level of threat had remained mostly at yellow, and had been raised several times to orange. As of late 2004, New York City had been on orange alert since the federal government set up the advisory system.

> "We must be willing to sacrifice a small measure of our liberties to preserve the great bulk of them."
>
> —*Clarence M. Kelley, director of the Federal Bureau of Investigation, August 9, 1975*

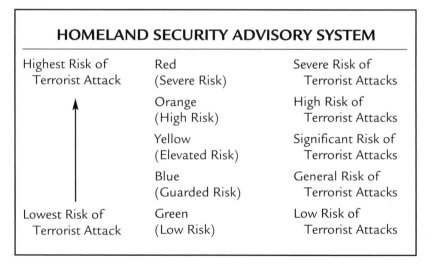

HOMELAND SECURITY ADVISORY SYSTEM

Highest Risk of Terrorist Attack	Red (Severe Risk)	Severe Risk of Terrorist Attacks
	Orange (High Risk)	High Risk of Terrorist Attacks
	Yellow (Elevated Risk)	Significant Risk of Terrorist Attacks
	Blue (Guarded Risk)	General Risk of Terrorist Attacks
Lowest Risk of Terrorist Attack	Green (Low Risk)	Low Risk of Terrorist Attacks

THE FUTURE OF AMERICAN LEGAL RIGHTS

The USA PATRIOT Act soon became the center of stormy debate. Civil liberties groups complained that the act trampled upon civil liberties. Such groups later began bringing court cases against the federal government to limit its newly expanded powers. Some of these cases may someday reach the U.S. Supreme Court. Years after the USA PATRIOT Act became law, it continued to stir debate. Civil liberties groups urged the U.S. Congress not to renew those parts of the act set to end in 2005. Some lawmakers (both Democratic and Republican) tried to restrict the USA PATRIOT Act. By early February 2004, the governments of 247 cities, towns, and counties and three states had passed resolutions (formal statements) opposing the USA PATRIOT Act. New York City, the site of the terrorist attacks against the World Trade Center on September 11, 2001, is one of the communities that passed a resolution against the act.

Meanwhile, the Bush administration sought to increase the powers of the federal government to carry out the law and gather intelligence. On the day before the second anniversary of the September 11 terrorist attacks, President Bush asked Congress to give police and prosecutors more powers to fight terrorism: Among other things, he wanted lawmakers to make terrorist crimes that result in death capital crimes, and to give the federal government the power to hold accused terrorists without bail and the power to subpoena records and witnesses without having to go to a judge or grand jury. Critics called the president's proposed list of powers "PATRIOT Act II." Also, during the State of the Union address (the president's yearly message to Congress) on January 20, 2004, President Bush called on Congress to renew the USA PATRIOT Act. He and other members of his administration also called for making the act permanent.

More than two years after the USA PATRIOT Act became law, most Americans still seemed to support it. For example, in a poll conducted by the Gallup Organization in February 2004, 43 percent of those questioned said that the USA PATRIOT Act is "about right," and that it does not limit civil liberties too much or too lit-

> "The ultimate aim of government is . . . to free every man from fear, that he may live in all possible security. . . . In fact, the true aim of government is liberty."
>
> —*Benedict Spinoza, Dutch philosopher, in* Theological-Political Treatise, *1670*

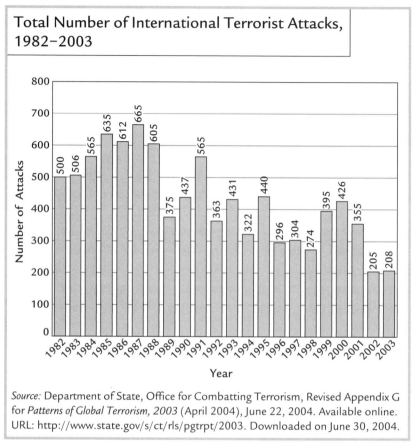

Total Number of International Terrorist Attacks, 1982–2003

Source: Department of State, Office for Combatting Terrorism, Revised Appendix G for *Patterns of Global Terrorism, 2003* (April 2004), June 22, 2004. Available online. URL: http://www.state.gov/s/ct/rls/pgtrpt/2003. Downloaded on June 30, 2004.

This graph shows the total number of terrorist attacks in the world from 1982 to 2003.

tle. In a poll conducted in April 2004 for CBS News and the *New York Times,* of those who had "heard a lot or some about the USA Patriot Act," 52 percent of those questioned said that it is "a necessary tool that helps the government find terrorists," and 42 percent said that it "is a threat to civil liberties." Both polls questioned more than 1,000 adults.

On the other hand, only a few Americans seemed to know a lot about the USA PATRIOT Act. For example, in the CBS News/*New York Times* poll, only 39 percent of those questioned had "heard or read about the USA Patriot Act," and only 12 percent had "read a lot about it." In the Gallup poll, only 13 percent of those questioned said that they were "very familiar" with the USA PATRIOT Act; 46 percent said that they were "somewhat familiar" with it.

Moreover, many seem confused about which powers the federal government gained under the USA PATRIOT Act. For example, 60 percent of those questioned in the Gallup poll wrongly believed that the USA PATRIOT Act gave government officials the power to hold people suspected of being terrorists for as long as the government wanted to do so "without charging them with a crime or allowing them access to a lawyer." In fact, President Bush based his power to hold "enemy combatants" indefinitely on the U.S. Constitution, which, in Article 2, Section 2, gives the president the power to serve as commander in chief of the armed forces.

Finally, when told about some sections of the act, many questioned in the Gallup poll found them troubling. For example, 71 percent disapproved of a part in the USA PATRIOT Act that increases the power of the federal government to use "sneak and peek" warrants. Such warrants allow law enforcement officers to delay notifying someone until after they have searched that person's property or belongings. For example, government officials can secretly enter and search someone's home with a search warrant when the homeowner is away, take pictures, and, in some cases, seize things without telling the person until later. To get a "sneak and peek" warrant, an official only has to show that notifying the person beforehand would put an investigation at risk. The U.S. Supreme Court has not yet said whether "sneak and peek" warrants are constitutional.

The debate over the USA PATRIOT Act represents the nation's struggle to balance freedom and security at a time when Americans have to confront global terrorism as an ever-present danger. As long as terrorism remains so, finding the right balance between freedom and national security will likely continue to be a major issue.

Glossary

accused Someone who has been arrested for or formally accused of a crime.

acquit To find a defendant who was accused of a crime not guilty.

arrest The holding and seizure of someone by or without force by someone (such as a police officer) acting under the power of law.

bail The money or property (or the promise of money or property) a defendant gives in return for being released from jail.

capital Punishable by death or involving an execution (such as capital punishment or a capital case).

case A word commonly used to refer to a lawsuit.

charge To accuse, especially in order to bring to trial; an accusation.

civil case A noncriminal lawsuit, for example, one involving a legal disagreement between two individuals.

compulsory process The legal means (such as a subpoena) used to force someone to appear in court in order to testify as a witness for the defense.

confront To face or bring a witness face-to-face with oneself, especially in order to challenge a witness's testimony by questioning.

convict To find a defendant guilty of a crime.

counsel A lawyer who helps try or manage a case in court. It is also a lawyer who is appointed or hired to advise or represent someone in legal matters.

crime   An illegal act that is seen as affecting the public, although only one person might have been harmed. Examples of crimes are murder, arson, burglary, and robbery.

damages   Money that a court orders the losing side to pay the winning side in a civil suit in order to make up for the winning side's loss or injury. In civil cases tried by a jury, the jury decides the amount of damages to be awarded.

death penalty   Death as punishment for a crime.

defendant   The accused or the person being sued in a civil case. In civil cases, the defendant can also be a group (such as a corporation).

double jeopardy   The trying of someone twice for the same crime.

due process   The right to be treated fairly under the law. For example, by law, the government cannot punish someone for a crime without a fair trial. See also procedural due process and substantive due process.

eminent domain   The power of the government to take private property for public use.

evidence   Something (such as testimony, writings, or objects) presented in court in order to prove whether a statement or supposed fact is true or false.

exclusionary rule   This rule says that evidence received by violating the constitutional rights of defendants cannot be used against them in criminal trials.

execute   To put to death in order to carry out a sentence of death.

fine   A sum of money that is to be paid, or something (such as money or property) that is given up or paid, as punishment.

frisk   To run one's hands quickly over the outer clothing of a suspect in order to find hidden weapons.

good faith exception   This exception to the exclusionary rule allows the government to use evidence obtained by an illegal search warrant against a defendant in a trial if the police reasonably believed at the time that the warrant was legal.

grand jury   A group of people chosen to examine the government's accusations against someone charged with a crime.

habeas corpus   A writ ordering that a prisoner be brought before the court so that it can decide whether the prisoner has been lawfully imprisoned. It also refers to the right of prisoners to get a writ of habeas corpus in order to protect themselves against being illegally imprisoned.

immunity   Freedom from being punished for a crime.

incriminate   To accuse of being involved in a crime, or to show evidence or proof of being involved in a crime.

indict   To charge with a crime.

indictment   A formal document that charges someone or a group of people with a crime. The prosecutor writes the indictment and presents it to a grand jury, which decides whether there is enough evidence to formally charge those named on the indictment with a crime.

information   A written accusation of a crime.

judge   A public official who has the power to hear and decide legal matters brought before a court.

juror   A member of a jury.

jury   A chosen group of people who have taken an oath to examine and decide matters of fact (such as in a trial).

just compensation   Fair payment for private property taken by the government for public use.

lawsuit (suit)   In a lawsuit, someone brings another to court for wrongdoing. In criminal lawsuits, prosecutors bring people to court for committing crimes. Civil lawsuits, which are brought by individuals or a group, such as a corporation, involve private rights. In these cases, someone (called the plaintiff) brings another (called the defendant) to court for wronging the plaintiff. The plaintiff wants the defendant to make up for the plaintiff's loss or to right the wrong done by the defendant to the plaintiff.

magistrate   A local court officer who has some of the powers of judges. A magistrate is also a local, state, or federal court officer who has the power to issue warrants.

***Miranda* rights**   Rights that people have when placed under arrest. *Miranda* rights include the right to remain silent; the right to have an attorney present during questioning; and the right, if one is poor, to be given a lawyer. The U.S. Supreme Court's decision in *Miranda v. Arizona* (1966) created these rights.

***Miranda* warnings**   A set of warnings that an arresting officer must give someone who has been arrested. *Miranda* warnings advise people under arrest of their *Miranda* rights.

petit jury   A group of usually 12 people who decide during a trial whether the accused is guilty or not guilty.

plaintiff   The one who brings a case to court. The plaintiff can also be a group (such as a corporation).

plea   The answer that defendants give to a formal charge that they have committed a crime. Defendants usually plead either guilty or not guilty.

presentment   A document that is like an indictment, except that the members of a grand jury make a presentment by choice, without an indictment laid before them; or, they make a presentment based on their own knowledge.

probable cause   A good reason (reason based on facts) for believing that (1) something illegal has been or is being done, (2) the person to be arrested is guilty of breaking the law, (3) the thing to be seized is in the place named on the warrant, or (4) a search will uncover illegal goods.

procedural due process   Legal actions that fairly and properly follow established rules and principles.

proceeding   An action or a series of actions done in order, for example, to carry out the law, to protect a right, or to correct a wrong. A trial is an example of a proceeding.

prosecute   To formally accuse someone suspected of committing a crime and to try to prove in court that the accused is guilty. Prosecutors (lawyers who act on behalf of the government) are responsible for prosecuting crimes.

public use   Any use that benefits the public at least generally.

seize   To take or take control of by the power of law.

self-incrimination   The act of incriminating oneself.

sentence   The punishment imposed by a court on someone who has been convicted; a formal decision by a court stating the punishment that someone who has been convicted will receive.

subpoena   A writ ordering someone to appear (such as in court or before a congressional committee). The order warns that the person will be punished if he or she fails to appear.

substantive due process   The requirement that laws involve a proper government interest and that they not result in unfair or unjust treatment of individuals.

sue   To bring a case to court.

testify   To give testimony.

testimony   An oral or a written statement made under oath by a witness, especially in a court.

trial   A legal proceeding where a judge hears and decides legal matters brought in court.

try   To conduct the trial of or to put on trial. Also, to examine or investigate facts, for example, in a court.

unreasonable   Not having a good legal reason. Specifically, *unreasonable* describes a government search or seizure that is not supported by a warrant when one is legally required.

verdict   A jury decision or the amount awarded in a jury decision in a civil case.

warrant   A writ giving an officer the power to do something that is necessary in order to carry out the law. For example, a judge may issue a warrant that gives an officer the power to search someone's home.

witness   Someone who testifies or gives evidence in court.

writ   A written legal order.

Chronology

1215

- *June 15:* King John of England accepts Magna Carta. By the end of the 14th century, Magna Carta becomes the basic source of English constitutional rights.

1354

- An act of the English Parliament restating Magna Carta is the first statute to use the phrase "due process of law."

1606

- *April 10:* King James I of England grants a charter to the London Company to set up a colony in Virginia. The Virginia Charter of 1606 is the first English royal charter to set up a permanent settlement in America.

1628

- *June 7:* King Charles I of England accepts the Petition of Right, the English Parliament's statement of complaints against King Charles I and of rights against the Crown.

1641

- *July 5:* England abolishes the Courts of High Commission and Star Chamber, and the oath *ex officio.*
- *December:* The Massachusetts legislature approves the Massachusetts Body of Liberties.

1679

♦ *May 26:* King Charles II of England accepts the Habeas Corpus Act, which defends the right to the writ of habeas corpus.

1689

♦ *December 16:* The English monarchs William III and Mary II accept the English Bill of Rights, which makes the English Parliament supreme over the Crown. The English Bill of Rights is the source of the Eighth Amendment.

1761

♦ *February:* James Otis, Jr., attacks Great Britain's use of writs of assistance in America in *Paxton's Case.*

1776

♦ *June 12:* Virginia adopts the Virginia Declaration of Rights, which will become the model for the Bill of Rights.
♦ *July 4:* The Continental Congress approves the Declaration of Independence.

1788

♦ *June 21:* The United States adopts the U.S. Constitution.

1791

♦ *December 15:* The United States adopts the Bill of Rights.

1833

♦ *February 16:* The U.S. Supreme Court says in *Barron v. City of Baltimore* that the Bill of Rights limits the power of the national government, not that of the states.

1868

♦ *July 9:* The United States adopts the Fourteenth Amendment. Over the next 100 years, the U.S. Supreme Court will say that the Fourteenth Amendment's due process clause forbids the states from violating certain rights protected by the Bill of Rights. Today, nearly all of the Bill of Rights applies to state and local governments.

1884

◆ *March 3:* The U.S. Supreme Court says in *Hurtado v. California* that a state criminal trial based on an information rather than an indictment by a grand jury does not violate the due process clause of the Fourteenth Amendment.

1914

◆ *February 24:* The U.S. Supreme Court establishes the exclusionary rule in *Weeks v. United States.*

1938

◆ *May 23:* The U.S. Supreme Court says in *Johnson v. Zerbst* that poor defendants have the right to be given a lawyer in federal criminal cases.
◆ *May 26:* The U.S. House of Representatives creates the House Un-American Activities Committee (HUAC), which will focus on exposing Communism in America.

1947

◆ *July 26:* The U.S. Congress passes the National Security Act. Part of the act creates the Central Intelligence Agency, whose mission is to gather foreign intelligence.

1949

◆ *June 27:* The U.S. Supreme Court says in *Wolf v. Colorado* that the due process clause of the Fourteenth Amendment guarantees people the Fourth Amendment right against unreasonable searches and seizures by state governments. The Court, however, says that the Fourteenth Amendment does not require the states to follow the exclusionary rule in state criminal trials. In *Mapp v. Ohio* (1961), the Court will reverse its position on the exclusionary rule.

1954

◆ *May 17:* The U.S. Supreme Court says in *Bolling v. Sharpe* that public school segregation in the District of Columbia deprives African-American children of liberty without due process. The Court hears this case with the four cases known as *Brown v. Board of Education.* Its decision will outlaw segregation in state public schools.

- *December 2:* The U.S. Senate condemns Wisconsin senator Joseph R. McCarthy, who rose to power by claiming that Communists were working in the federal government.

1955

- *May 23:* The U.S. Supreme Court says in *Quinn v. United States* that the Fifth Amendment guarantees witnesses the right against self-incrimination in legislative investigations.

1959

- *March 30:* The U.S. Supreme Court says in *Bartkus v. Illinois* and *Abbate v. United States* that the federal government and a state government can prosecute the same defendant for the same crime.

1961

- *June 19:* The U.S. Supreme Court says in *Mapp v. Ohio* that the states must follow the exclusionary rule in state criminal trials.

1963

- *March 18:* The U.S. Supreme Court says in *Gideon v. Wainwright* that poor defendants have the right to be given a lawyer in state criminal trials. Also, the Court says, for the first time, that the right to a lawyer is fundamental to a fair trial.

1966

- *June 13:* The U.S. Supreme Court says in *Miranda v. Arizona* that law enforcement officers must inform suspects that are under arrest that they have the right to remain silent and to have a lawyer present during questioning.

1967

- *December 18:* The U.S. Supreme Court says in *Katz v. United States* that the main purpose of the Fourth Amendment is to protect privacy, not property.

1968

- *June 10:* The U.S. Supreme Court says in *Terry v. Ohio* that law enforcement officers can stop and frisk someone who is acting suspiciously, even though they do not have probable cause to arrest that person.

1969

♦ *June 23:* The U.S. Supreme Court says in *Chimel v. California* that searches "incident to arrest" are limited to the area within the suspect's "immediate control" (meaning, the area from where the suspect may get a weapon or evidence that can be destroyed).

1970

♦ *June 22:* The U.S. Supreme Court says in *Williams v. Florida* that the Sixth Amendment right to trial by jury does not require a jury to have 12 people. Eight years later, the Court will say that the U.S. Constitution requires a jury to have at least six people. The Court also says in *Baldwin v. New York* that the U.S. Constitution does not require trial by jury in state trials for those accused of petty crimes.

1972

♦ *May 22:* The U.S. Supreme Court says in *Johnson v. Louisiana,* a case involving a conviction based on a verdict agreed to by nine of 12 jurors, that a conviction based on a verdict agreed to by less than all the members of a jury in a state criminal trial does not violate the due process and equal protection clauses of the Fourteenth Amendment. The Court also says in *Apodaca v. Oregon* that a conviction based on a verdict agreed to by less than all the members of the jury in a state criminal trial does not violate the defendant's right under the Sixth and Fourteenth Amendments to a trial by jury.

♦ *June 19:* The U.S. Supreme Court says in *United States v. United States District Court* that the Fourth Amendment requires the federal government to get a warrant in order to spy within the United States. In 2001, the U.S. Congress will give the federal government more power to spy on Americans in the USA PATRIOT Act.

♦ *June 29:* The U.S. Supreme Court says in *Furman v. Georgia* that capital punishment as currently practiced is unconstitutional because the death penalty is imposed randomly and unfairly.

1974

- *January 8:* The U.S. Supreme Court says in *United States v. Calandra* that prosecutors can admit illegally obtained evidence in grand jury proceedings.
- *August 9:* U.S. president Richard M. Nixon resigns from office because of the Watergate affair, a series of scandals involving, among other things, illegal wiretapping of citizens by the Nixon administration and political spying by the president's reelection committee.

1976

- *July 2:* The U.S. Supreme Court says in *Gregg v. Georgia* that the death penalty does not, in all circumstances, violate the right against "cruel and unusual punishments."

1978

- *March 21:* The U.S. Supreme Court says in *Ballew v. Georgia* that a jury of fewer than six people in a criminal trial violates the defendant's right, under the Sixth and Fourteenth Amendments, to trial by jury.

1979

- *April 17:* The U.S. Supreme Court says in *Burch v. Louisiana* that in a state trial concerning a nonpetty crime, a conviction based on a 5-1 verdict by a six-person jury violates the defendant's right to trial by jury under the Sixth and Fourteenth Amendments.

1980

- *July 2:* The U.S. Supreme Court says in *Richmond Newspapers, Inc., v. Virginia* that, except in special cases, the public and the press have the right under the First and Fourteenth Amendments to attend criminal trials and to publish information about them, even in cases where the accused would like to give up their right to a public trial.

1981

- *January 26:* The U.S. Supreme Court says in *Chandler v. Florida* that states can allow television cameras, photo cameras, and radio microphones in the courtroom as long as the media can report the news without denying the defendant a fair trial.

1984

- *June 12:* The U.S. Supreme Court says in *New York v. Quarles* that a police officer does not have to give a suspect *Miranda* warnings before questioning if the officer is reasonably concerned for public safety.
- *July 5:* The U.S. Supreme Court establishes the "good faith" exception to the exclusionary rule in *United States v. Leon:* In cases where a search warrant is later found illegal by a higher court, the government can use the evidence that was obtained under the warrant against the defendant in a trial if the police reasonably believed at the time that the warrant was legal. The good faith exception will become the most important exception to the exclusionary rule.

1988

- *June 29:* The U.S. Supreme Court says in *Thompson v. Oklahoma* that executing people who were less than 16 years old when they committed the crime violates the Eighth Amendment's ban against cruel and unusual punishments.

1989

- *June 26:* The U.S. Supreme Court says in *Stanford v. Kentucky* that teenagers who are at least 16 years old can receive the death penalty.

2001

- *September 11:* Al-Qaeda terrorists hijack airplanes and crash them into the World Trade Center towers in New York City and the Pentagon in Washington, D.C. A fourth plane, probably heading for another target in Washington, D.C., crashes in a field near Shanksville, Pennsylvania.
- *October 7:* The United States and Great Britain attack Afghanistan, beginning the war to overthrow the Taliban and to destroy al-Qaeda.
- *October 8:* U.S. president George W. Bush issues an order creating the Office of Homeland Security.
- *October 26:* U.S. president George W. Bush signs the USA PATRIOT Act into law.
- *December 7:* The Taliban surrenders Kandahar, the Taliban's base of power in Afghanistan and the last city under the Taliban's control, to the United States and its allies.

2002

- *January:* U.S. forces and their allies have mostly defeated the Taliban and al-Qaeda in Afghanistan.
- *January 10:* The United States flies the first group of prisoners out of Afghanistan to a prison camp at Guantánamo Bay, Cuba. The U.S. government declares that the prisoners are "unlawful combatants" and denies they have the traditional rights of prisoners of war.
- *May 8:* U.S. officers arrest Jose Padilla at the O'Hare International Airport in Chicago, Illinois, where he arrived from Pakistan. The United States claims that Padilla was plotting with members of al-Qaeda to build and set off a radioactive bomb in the United States. The government holds Padilla as an enemy combatant.
- *May 14:* U.S. president George W. Bush signs the Enhanced Border Security and Visa Entry Reform Act, which seeks to prevent suspected terrorists from entering the country. The act requires increased border checks and closer tracking of foreign students. The act also requires all passports issued to foreign visitors after 2003 to contain biometric identifiers, such as fingerprints or a facial image that can be scanned.
- *June 20:* The U.S. Supreme Court says in *Atkins v. Virginia* that executing mentally retarded people violates the Eighth Amendment's ban against "cruel and unusual punishments."
- *November 25:* U.S. president George W. Bush signs the Department of Homeland Security Act into law. The act reclassifies the Office of Homeland Security as a federal department.

2004

- *January 5:* The Department of Homeland Security announces the United States Visitor and Immigrant Status Indicator Technology (US-VISIT), which uses biometrics to track the travel of foreign visitors to and from the United States.
- *June 28:* The U.S. Supreme Court says in *Hamdi v. Rumsfeld* and *Rasul v. Bush* that prisoners who are "enemy combatants" have the right to challenge their imprisonment in court.

2005

- *March 1:* The U.S. Supreme Court says in *Roper v. Simmons* that executing people who were under 18 years old when they committed their crimes violates the right against cruel and unusual punishments under the Eighth and Fourteenth Amendments.

Appendix

Excerpts from Documents Relating to Legal Rights

Magna Carta, June 15, 1215

Influenced by English thinkers, such as Sir Edward Coke, Americans in the 17th and 18th centuries traced many of the rights later guaranteed by the Bill of Rights to Magna Carta and considered the rights guaranteed by it to be a common law birthright. Chapter 39 is a direct forerunner of the due process clause of the Fifth Amendment. Americans in the 17th and 18th centuries also traced the right against unreasonable seizures and the right to trial by jury to chapter 39 (although "the lawful judgment of his peers" did not actually mean "trial by jury"). Scholars have also traced the right to a speedy trial to chapter 40. Chapters 20 to 22, which forbid excessive fines for free men, remind one of the Eighth Amendment's ban against excessive fines. Chapters 28 through 31 forbid royal officials from taking private property without payment, or in other cases, without the owner's consent. Under the Fifth Amendment, the government cannot take "private property . . . for public use, without just compensation." Below are excerpts from these key chapters.

20. A freeman shall be amerced for a small offence only according to the degree of the offence; and for a grave offence he shall be amerced

according to the gravity of the offence, saving his contenement. And a merchant shall be amerced in the same way, saving his merchandise; and a villein in the same way, saving his wainage—should they fall into our mercy. And none of the aforesaid amercements shall be imposed except by the oaths of good men from the neighbourhood.

21. Earls and barons shall be amerced only by their peers, and only according to the degree of the misdeed.

22. No clergyman shall be amerced with respect to his lay tenement except in the manner of those aforesaid, not according to the value of his ecclesiastical benefice. . . .

28. No constable or other bailiff of ours shall take grain or other chattels of any one without immediate payment therefor in money, unless by the will of the seller he may secure postponement of that [payment].

29. No constable shall distrain any knight to pay money for castle-guard when he is willing to perform that service himself, or through another good man if for reasonable cause he is unable to perform it himself. And if we lead or send him on a military expedition, he shall be quit of [castle-]guard for so long a time as he shall be with the army at our command.

30. No sheriff or bailiff of ours, nor any other person, shall take the horses or carts of any freeman for carrying service, except by the will of that freeman.

31. Neither we nor our bailiffs will take some one else's wood for [repairing] castles or for doing any other work of ours, except by the will of him to whom the wood belongs. . . .

39. No freemen shall be captured or imprisoned or disseised or outlawed or exiled or in any way destroyed, nor will we go against him or send against him, except by the lawful judgment of his peers or by the law of the land.

40. To no one will we sell, to no one will we deny or delay right or justice.

Source: Bernard Schwartz, comp., *Roots of the Bill of Rights,* 5 vols.
(New York: Chelsea House, 1980), pp. 10–12.

Petition of Right, June 7, 1628

The Petition of Right, which declared that subjects have rights against the Crown, restated chapter 39 of Magna Carta and the 1354 act that restated Magna Carta. The 1354 act was the first statute to use the phrase "due process of law." The petition also supported due process by condemning putting subjects in prison without giving legal reasons and supporting the right to the writ of habeas corpus. The framers of the U.S. Constitution also considered the rights that the English Parliament declared in the Petition of Right to be their common law birthright. In the below excerpt, "the Great Charter of the Liberties of England" refers to Magna Carta.

And where also, by the statute called the Great Charter of the Liberties of England, it is declared and enacted that no freeman may be taken or imprisoned, or be disseised of his freehold or liberties or his free customs, or be outlawed or exiled or in any manner destroyed, but by the lawful judgment of his peers or by the law of the land; and in the eight-and-twentieth year of the reign of King Edward III it was declared and enacted by authority of parliament that no man, of what estate or condition that he be, should be put out of his land or tenements, nor taken, nor imprisoned, nor disherited, nor put to death, without being brought to answer by due process of law: nevertheless, against the tenor of the said statutes and other the good laws and statutes of your realm to that end provided, divers of your subjects have of late been imprisoned without any cause showed; and when for their deliverance they were brought before your justices by your majesty's writs of *habeas corpus,* there to undergo and receive as the court should order, and their keepers commanded to certify the causes of their detainer, no cause was certified, but that they were detained by your majesty's special command, signified by the lords of your privy council; and yet were returned back to several prisons, without being charged with anything to which they might make answer according to the law. . . .

They do therefore humbly pray your most excellent majesty . . . that no freeman, in any such manner as is before mentioned, be imprisoned or detained.

Source: Bernard Schwartz, comp., *Roots of the Bill of Rights,* 5 vols.
(New York: Chelsea House, 1980), pp. 20–21.

English Bill of Rights, December 16, 1689

The framers of the U.S. Constitution considered the rights guaranteed by the English Bill of Rights, along with those guaranteed by Magna Carta and the Petition of Right, their common law birthright. The English Bill of Rights made the English Parliament supreme over the Crown. One of the clauses in the English Bill of Rights is the direct forerunner of the Eighth Amendment. The following clause is also a forerunner of the right to trial by jury.

. . . that excessive bail ought not to be required, nor excessive fines imposed, nor cruel and unusual punishments inflicted; that jurors ought to be duly impanelled and returned, and jurors which pass upon men in trials for high treason ought to be freeholders. . . .

Source: Bernard Schwartz, comp., *Roots of the Bill of Rights,* 5 vols.
(New York: Chelsea House, 1980), p. 43.

Virginia Declaration of Rights, June 12, 1776

During the American Revolution, Virginia was the first colony to adopt a declaration of rights and a constitution. James Madison used the Virginia Declaration of Rights as a model when he wrote the amendments that became the Bill of Rights. The declaration guaranteed many of the rights now guaranteed in the Fourth through Eighth Amendments of the Bill of Rights. Section 8 of the declaration guaranteed the accused the right to know the charges against them, "to be confronted with the accusers and witnesses," and "to call for evidence in [their] favor"; the right "to a speedy trial by . . . jury"; and the right against self-incrimination. Section 8 also guaranteed the right to due process. The Eighth Amendment restates section 9 of the declaration nearly word for word. Both the Eighth Amendment and section 9 come directly from the English Bill of Rights. As does the Fourth Amendment, section 10 of the declaration outlawed general warrants. Section 11 guaranteed the right to trial by jury in civil cases. Below are excerpts from these sections.

Section 8. That in all capital or criminal prosecutions a man has a right to demand the cause and nature of his accusation, to be confronted with the accusers and witnesses, to call for evidence in his favor, and

to a speedy trial by an impartial jury of twelve men of his vicinage [neighborhood], without whose unanimous consent he cannot be found guilty; nor can he be compelled to give evidence against himself; that no man be deprived of his liberty except by the law of the land or the judgment of his peers.

Section 9. That excessive bail ought not to be required, nor excessive fines imposed, nor cruel and unusual punishments inflicted.

Section 10. That general warrants, whereby an officer or messenger may be commanded to search suspected places without evidence of a fact committed, or to seize any person or persons not named, or whose offense is not particularly described and supported by evidence, are grievous and oppressive and ought not to be granted.

Section 11. That in controversies respecting property, and in suits between man and man, the ancient trial by jury is preferable to any other and ought to be held sacred.

Source: National Archives and Records Administration, "The Virginia Declaration of Rights," National Archives and Records Administration. Available online. URL: http://www.archives.gov/national_archives_experience/ charters/virginia_declaration_of_rights.html. Downloaded on August 5, 2004.

Declaration of Independence, July 4, 1776

By 1776, the American colonists lost all hope that they could settle their differences with Great Britain peacefully and remain part of the British Empire. In May, the Continental Congress called for the colonies to set up their own governments. The next month, the Continental Congress adopted the Declaration of Independence. In the declaration, the Americans defended their decision to break with Britain by listing rights that, according to the Americans, the British Crown had violated. The declaration accused Britain's king George III of trying to establish "an absolute tyranny over these states." One example of such "tyranny" was "depriving us, in many cases, of the benefits of trial by jury." The Declaration of Independence is now considered to be the most important American historical document. The chief writer of the declaration, Thomas Jefferson, became the third president of the United States in 1801. Below is a short excerpt.

. . . For depriving us in many cases, of the benefits of Trial by Jury: For transporting us beyond Seas to be tried for pretended offences. . . .

Bill of Rights, December 15, 1791

The Fourth through Eighth Amendments of the Bill of Rights limit the power of government to invade or take away people's privacy or property, and requires the government to treat people fairly under the law. The Fourth Amendment guarantees the right against unreasonable searches and seizures. The Fifth Amendment guarantees the right to indictment by a grand jury, the right against double jeopardy, the right against self-incrimination, the right to due process, and the right to just compensation. The Sixth Amendment guarantees the accused the right to a speedy trial, the right to a public trial, the right to a trial by jury, the right to know the charges against them, the right to confront the witnesses against them, the right to call witnesses for their defense, and the right to counsel. The Seventh Amendment guarantees defendants the right to trial by jury in civil cases. The Eighth Amendment guarantees the right against excessive bail or fines, and the right against cruel and unusual punishments. Below are excerpts.

AMENDMENT IV

The right of the people to be secure in their persons, houses, papers, and effects, against unreasonable searches and seizures, shall not be violated, and no Warrants shall issue, but upon probable cause, supported by Oath or affirmation, and particularly describing the place to be searched, and the persons or things to be seized.

AMENDMENT V

No person shall be held to answer for a capital, or otherwise infamous crime, unless on a presentment or indictment of a Grand July, except in cases arising in the land or naval forces, or in the Militia, when in actual service in time of War or public danger; nor shall any person be subject for the same offence to be twice put in jeopardy of life or limb; nor shall be compelled in any criminal case to be a witness against himself, nor be deprived of life, liberty, or property, without due process of law; nor shall private property be taken for public use, without just compensation.

AMENDMENT VI

In all criminal prosecutions, the accused shall enjoy the right to a speedy and public trial, by an impartial jury of the State and district wherein the crime shall have been committed, which district shall have been previously ascertained by law, and to be informed of the nature and cause of the accusation; to be confronted with the witnesses against him; to have compulsory process for obtaining witnesses in his favor, and to have the Assistance of Counsel for his defence.

AMENDMENT VII

In suits at common law, where the value in controversy shall exceed twenty dollars, the right of trial by jury shall be preserved, and no fact tried by a jury, shall be otherwise reexamined in any Court of the United States, than according to the rules of the common law.

AMENDMENT VIII

Excessive bail shall not be required, nor excessive fines imposed, nor cruel and unusual punishments inflicted.

Source: National Archives and Records Administration, "The Bill of Rights: A Transcription," National Archives and Records Administration. Available online. URL: http://www.archives.gov/national_archives_experience/ charters/bill_of_rights_transcript.html. Downloaded on July 28, 2004.

Bolling v. Sharpe, May 17, 1954

The U.S. Supreme Court applied the principle of substantive due process to the issue of discrimination in *Bolling v. Sharpe* (1954). In *Bolling,* the Court was asked to decide whether racial segregation of public schoolchildren in Washington, D.C., violated the due process clause of the Fifth Amendment. The Court heard *Bolling* with the four cases now known as *Brown v. Board of Education* (1954). In *Brown,* the Court said that segregating children in state public schools by race violated the equal protection clause of the Fourteenth Amendment. The Court gave a separate opinion on *Bolling v. Sharpe* because the Fourteenth Amendment applies only to the states and thus not to the District of Columbia.

The Court found that public school segregation in the District of Columbia violated the Fifth Amendment's due process clause, even though the amendment does not contain an equal protection clause. According to the Court, school segregation was "not reasonably related to any proper" government goal; therefore, barring black children from attending public schools attended by white children deprived black children of liberty without due process. Below are excerpts from the Court opinion in *Bolling*.

MR. CHIEF JUSTICE WARREN delivered the opinion of the Court. . . .

We have this day held that the Equal Protection Clause of the Fourteenth Amendment prohibits the states from maintaining racially segregated public schools. The legal problem in the District of Columbia is somewhat different, however. The Fifth Amendment, which is applicable in the District of Columbia, does not contain an equal protection clause as does the Fourteenth Amendment which applies only to the states. But the concepts of equal protection and due process, both stemming from our American ideal of fairness, are not mutually exclusive. The "equal protection of the laws" is a more explicit safeguard of prohibited unfairness than "due process of law," and, therefore, we do not imply that the two are always interchangeable phrases. But, as this Court has recognized, discrimination may be so unjustifiable as to be violative of due process.

Classifications based solely upon race must be scrutinized with particular care, since they are contrary to our traditions and hence constitutionally suspect. . . .

Although the Court has not assumed to define "liberty" with any great precision, that term is not confined to mere freedom from bodily restraint. Liberty under law extends to the full range of conduct which the individual is free to pursue, and it cannot be restricted except for a proper governmental objective. Segregation in public education is not reasonably related to any proper governmental objective, and thus it imposes on Negro children of the District of Columbia a burden that constitutes an arbitrary deprivation of their liberty in violation of the Due Process Clause.

In view of our decision that the Constitution prohibits the states from maintaining racially segregated public schools, it would be unthinkable that the same Constitution would impose a lesser duty on the Federal Government. We hold that racial segregation in the public schools of the District of Columbia is a denial of the due process of law guaranteed by the Fifth Amendment to the Constitution.

Source: Bolling v. Sharpe, 347 U.S. 497 (1954).

Mapp v. Ohio, June 19, 1961

In *Weeks v. United States* (1914), the U.S. Supreme Court said that the Fourth Amendment bars the government from using evidence obtained from an illegal search or seizure by federal officers. This decision established the exclusionary rule, which bars evidence obtained by violating the constitutional rights of defendants. The Court said, however, that the exclusionary rule applied only to federal, not state, criminal cases. In *Wolf v. Colorado* (1949), the Court barred the states from violating the Fourth Amendment right against unreasonable searches and seizures. But the Court still refused to require the states to follow the exclusionary rule. In *Mapp v. Ohio* (1961), however, the Court reversed itself and said that the exclusionary rule also applies to the states.

The Court has since limited the exclusionary rule in important ways. For example, in *Harris v. New York* (1971), the Court allowed prosecutors to use illegally obtained evidence to challenge a defendant's testimony in court. In *United States v. Calandra* (1974), the Court allowed prosecutors to admit illegally obtained evidence in grand jury proceedings. The most important exception to the exclusionary rule is the "good faith" exception, which the Court established in *United States v. Leon* (1984). In cases where a search warrant is found later by a higher court to be illegal, the good faith exception allows the government to use the evidence that was obtained under the warrant against the defendant in a trial if the police reasonably believed at the time that the warrant was legal. Below are excerpts from the Court opinion in *Mapp.*

MR. JUSTICE CLARK delivered the opinion of the Court. . . .

The State says that even if the search were made without authority, or otherwise unreasonably, it is not prevented from using the unconstitutionally seized evidence at trial, citing *Wolf v. Colorado,* 338 U.S. 25 (1949), in which this Court did indeed hold "that in a prosecution in a State court for a State crime the Fourteenth Amendment does not forbid the admission of evidence obtained by an unreasonable search and seizure." . . .

. . . Today we once again examine *Wolf's* constitutional documentation of the right to privacy free from unreasonable state intrusion, and, after its dozen years on our books, are led by it to close the only courtroom door remaining open to evidence secured by official lawlessness in flagrant abuse of that basic right, reserved to all persons as a specific guarantee against that very same unlawful conduct. We hold that all evidence obtained by searches and seizures in violation of the Constitution is, by that same authority, inadmissible in a state court.

Since the Fourth Amendment's right of privacy has been declared enforceable against the States through the Due Process Clause of the Fourteenth, it is enforceable against them by the same sanction of exclusion as is used against the Federal Government. Were it otherwise, then just as without the *Weeks* rule the assurance against unreasonable federal searches and seizures would be "a form of words," valueless and undeserving of mention in a perpetual charter of inestimable human liberties, so too, without that rule the freedom from state invasions of privacy would be so ephemeral and so neatly severed from its conceptual nexus with the freedom from all brutish means of coercing evidence as not to merit this Court's high regard as a freedom "implicit in the concept of ordered liberty." . . . in extending the substantive protections of due process to all constitutionally unreasonable searches—state or federal—it was logically and constitutionally necessary that the exclusion doctrine—an essential part of the right to privacy—be also insisted upon as an essential ingredient of the right newly recognized by the *Wolf* case. . . .

. . . our holding that the exclusionary rule is an essential part of both the Fourth and Fourteenth Amendments is not only the logical dictate of prior cases, but it also makes very good sense. There is no war between the Constitution and common sense. Presently, a federal prosecutor may make no use of evidence illegally seized, but a State's attorney across the street may, although he supposedly is operating under the enforceable prohibitions of the same Amendment. Thus the State, by admitting evidence unlawfully seized, serves to encourage disobedience to the Federal Constitution which it is bound to uphold. . . .

There are those who say, as did Justice (then Judge) Cardozo, that under our constitutional exclusionary doctrine "[t]he criminal is to go free because the constable has blundered." . . . In some cases this will undoubtedly be the result. . . . The criminal goes free, if he must, but it is the law that sets him free. Nothing can destroy a government more quickly than its failure to observe its own laws, or worse, its disregard of the charter of its own existence.

Source: Mapp v. Ohio, 367 U.S. 643 (1961).

Gideon v. Wainwright, March 18, 1963

Until the 20th century, the U.S. Supreme Court assumed that the Sixth Amendment did not guarantee poor defendants the right to be assigned a lawyer. In *Johnson v. Zerbst* (1938), the Court said that poor defendants have the right to be given a lawyer in federal criminal cases. Concerning state criminal cases, however, the Court said in *Betts v. Brady* (1942) that not providing lawyers for poor defendants in noncapital cases did not deny them a fair trial, as required by due process of law under the Fourteenth Amendment. In *Gideon v. Wainwright,* the Court overturned its decision in *Betts.* Most important, for the first time, the Court said that the right to a lawyer is fundamental to a fair trial. Below are excerpts from the Court opinion in *Gideon.*

MR. JUSTICE BLACK delivered the opinion of the Court. . . .

. . . Since 1942, when *Betts v. Brady,* 316 U.S. 455, was decided by a divided Court, the problem of a defendant's federal constitutional right to counsel in a state court has been a continuing source of controversy and litigation in both state and federal courts. . . .

. . . It was held [in *Betts*] that a refusal to appoint counsel for an indigent defendant charged with a felony did not necessarily violate the Due Process Clause of the Fourteenth Amendment, which for reasons given the Court deemed to be the only applicable federal constitutional provision. . . .

. . . we think the *Betts v. Brady* holding if left standing would require us to reject Gideon's claim that the Constitution guarantees him the assistance of counsel. Upon full reconsideration we conclude that *Betts v. Brady* should be overruled. . . .

. . . reason and reflection require us to recognize that in our adversary system of criminal justice, any person haled into court, who is too poor to hire a lawyer, cannot be assured a fair trial unless counsel is provided for him. This seems to us to be an obvious truth. . . . From the very beginning, our state and national constitutions and laws have laid great emphasis on procedural and substantive safeguards designed to assure fair trials before impartial tribunals in which every defendant stands equal before the law. This noble ideal cannot be realized if the poor man charged with crime has to face his accusers without a lawyer to assist him.

Source: Gideon v. Wainwright, 372 U.S. 335 (1963).

Miranda v. Arizona, June 13, 1966

Before 1966, someone being questioned by the police had to claim the right against self-incrimination if he or she wanted to be protected by the right. As interpreted by earlier U.S. Supreme Court decisions, the self-incrimination clause did not bar unforced confessions or other incriminating statements from being used as evidence in trials. Also, police officers did not have to warn suspects that they had a right not to answer questions, and suspects did not have the right to have a lawyer present during police questioning.

In *Miranda v. Arizona,* the Court sought to ensure that suspects who made incriminating statements did so voluntarily. The Court outlined a set of warnings that the police must give people who have been arrested. These warnings, known as *Miranda* warnings, advise people under arrest that they have the right to remain silent and to have a lawyer present during questioning.

The Court has since eased the limits *Miranda* placed on law enforcement officers. For example, in *New York v. Quarles* (1984), the Court said that a police officer does not have to give a suspect *Miranda* warnings before questioning if the officer is reasonably concerned for public safety. Below are excerpts from the Court opinion in *Miranda.*

MR. CHIEF JUSTICE WARREN delivered the opinion of the Court.

The cases before us raise questions which go to the roots of our concepts of American criminal jurisprudence: the restraints society must observe consistent with the Federal Constitution in prosecuting individuals for crime. More specifically, we deal with the admissibility of statements obtained from an individual who is subjected to custodial police interrogation and the necessity for procedures which assure that the individual is accorded his privilege under the Fifth Amendment to the Constitution not to be compelled to incriminate himself. . . .

. . . We have concluded that without proper safeguards the process of in-custody interrogation of persons suspected or accused of crime contains inherently compelling pressures which work to undermine the individual's will to resist and to compel him to speak where he would not otherwise do so freely. In order to combat these pressures and to permit a full opportunity to exercise the privilege against self-incrimination, the accused must be adequately and effectively apprised of his rights and the exercise of those rights must be fully honored. . . .

. . . we hold that when an individual is taken into custody or otherwise deprived of his freedom by the authorities in any significant way and is subjected to questioning, the privilege against self-incrimination is jeopardized. Procedural safeguards must be employed to protect the privilege, and unless other fully effective means are adopted to notify the person of his right of silence and to assure that the exercise of the right will be scrupulously honored, the following measures are required. He must be warned prior to any questioning that he has the right to remain silent, that anything he says can be used against him in a court of law, that he has the right to the presence of an attorney, and that if he cannot afford an attorney one will be appointed for him prior to any questioning if he so desires. Opportunity to exercise these rights must be afforded to him throughout the interrogation. After such warnings have been given, and such opportunity afforded him, the individual may knowingly and intelligently waive these rights and agree to answer questions or make a statement. But unless and until such warnings and waiver are demonstrated by the prosecution at trial, no evidence obtained as a result of interrogation can be used against him.

Source: Miranda v. Arizona, 384 U.S. 436 (1966).

Katz v. United States, December 18, 1967

Before 1967, the U.S. Supreme Court believed that the Fourth Amendment was meant to protect property interests. Thus, in *Olmstead v. United States* (1928), the Court found that wiretapping was not a search or a seizure within the meaning of the Fourth Amendment; therefore, the government did not need a warrant in order to wiretap someone's telephone conversations, as long as the government did not physically enter the person's property without permission or by force. Warrantless wiretapping continued to be legal until the Court's decision in *Katz v. United States* (1967). In *Katz,* the Court said that the main purpose of the Fourth Amendment is to protect privacy, not property. Thus, overruling its decision in 1928, the Court said that the Fourth Amendment requires the government to get a search warrant to install a wiretap.

In a separate opinion, Justice John Marshall Harlan argued that in certain situations, "a person has a constitutionally protected reasonable expectation of privacy." Since *Katz,* whether a search or seizure violates a "reasonable expectation of privacy" has determined whether a search or seizure is presumed to require a warrant. Now, however, the Court also tries to determine whether the expectation of privacy is so great that a search or seizure requires a warrant. Below are excerpts from the Court opinion in *Katz*.

MR. JUSTICE STEWART delivered the opinion of the Court. . . .

. . . the Fourth Amendment protects people, not places. What a person knowingly exposes to the public, even in his own home or office, is not a subject of Fourth Amendment protection. . . . But what he seeks to preserve as private, even in an area accessible to the public, may be constitutionally protected. . . .

The Government stresses the fact that the telephone booth from which the petitioner made his calls was constructed partly of glass, so that he was as visible after he entered it as he would have been if he had remained outside. But what he sought to exclude when he entered the booth was not the intruding eye—it was the uninvited ear. He did not shed his right to do so simply because he made his calls from a place where he might be seen. . . .

The Government contends, however, that the activities of its agents in this case should not be tested by Fourth Amendment requirements, for the surveillance technique they employed involved no physical penetration of the telephone booth from which the petitioner placed his calls. It is true that the absence of such penetration was at one time thought to foreclose further Fourth Amendment inquiry, . . . for that Amendment was thought to limit only searches and seizures of tangible property. But "[t]he premise that property interests control the right of the Government to search and seize has been discredited". . .

. . . The Government's activities in electronically listening to and recording the petitioner's words violated the privacy upon which he justifiably relied while using the telephone booth and thus constituted a "search and seizure" within the meaning of the Fourth Amendment. The fact that the electronic device employed to achieve that end did not happen to penetrate the wall of the booth can have no constitutional significance.

The question remaining for decision, then, is whether the search and seizure conducted in this case complied with constitutional standards. . . .

Accepting [the] account of the Government's actions as accurate, it is clear that this surveillance was so narrowly circumscribed that a duly authorized magistrate, properly notified of the need for such investigation, specifically informed of the basis on which it was to proceed, and clearly apprised of the precise intrusion it would entail, could constitutionally have authorized, with appropriate safeguards, the very limited search and seizure that the Government asserts in fact took place. . . .

The Government . . . argues that surveillance of a telephone booth should be exempted from the usual requirement of advance authorization by a magistrate upon a showing of probable cause. We cannot agree. Omission of such authorization

"bypasses the safeguards provided by an objective predetermination of probable cause, and substitutes instead the far less reliable procedure of an after-the-event justification for the . . . search, too likely to be subtly influenced by the familiar shortcomings of hindsight judgment." *Beck v. Ohio,* 379 U.S. 89, 96.

And bypassing a neutral predetermination of the scope of a search leaves individuals secure from Fourth Amendment violations "only in the discretion of the police". . . .

These considerations do not vanish when the search in question is transferred from the setting of a home, an office, or a hotel room to that of a telephone booth. Wherever a man may be, he is entitled to know that he will remain free from unreasonable searches and seizures.

Source: Katz v. United States, 389 U.S. 347 (1967).

Gregg v. Georgia, July 2, 1976

In *Furman v. Georgia* (1972), the U.S. Supreme Court said that capital punishment as then practiced was unconstitutional because the death penalty was imposed randomly and unfairly. *Furman* canceled the death penalty in the United States. The Court, however, stopped short of saying that the Eighth Amendment absolutely outlawed capital punishment. Instead, the Court challenged the U.S. Congress and the state legislatures to develop new statutes to ensure that the death penalty would be applied fairly. In *Gregg v. Georgia,* the Court allowed certain states to bring back capital punishment. Below are excerpts from the Court opinion in *Gregg.*

Judgment of the Court, and opinion of MR. JUSTICE STEWART, MR. JUSTICE POWELL, and MR. JUSTICE STEVENS, announced by MR. JUSTICE STEWART.

The issue in this case is whether the imposition of the sentence of death for the crime of murder under the law of Georgia violates the Eighth and Fourteenth Amendments. . . .

. . . until *Furman v. Georgia,* 408 U.S. 238 (1972), the Court never confronted squarely the fundamental claim that the punishment of death always, regardless of the enormity of the offense or the procedure followed in imposing the sentence, is cruel and unusual punishment in violation of the Constitution. Although this issue was presented and addressed in *Furman,* it was not resolved by the Court. Four Justices would have held that capital punishment is not unconstitutional per se; two Justices would have reached the opposite conclusion; and three Justices, while agreeing that the statutes then before the Court were invalid as applied, left open the question whether such punishment may ever be imposed. We now hold that the punishment of death does not invariably violate the Constitution. . . .

. . . in assessing a punishment selected by a democratically elected legislature against the constitutional measure, we presume its validity. We may not require the legislature to select the least severe penalty possible so long as the penalty selected is not cruelly inhumane or disproportionate to the crime involved. And a heavy burden rests on those who would attack the judgment of the representatives of the people. . . .

The imposition of the death penalty for the crime of murder has a long history of acceptance both in the United States and in England. The common-law rule imposed a mandatory death sentence on all convicted murderers. . . . And the penalty continued to be used into the 20th century by most American States. . . .

It is apparent from the text of the Constitution itself that the existence of capital punishment was accepted by the Framers. At the time the Eighth Amendment was ratified, capital punishment was a common sanction in every State. Indeed, the First Congress of the United States enacted legislation providing death as the penalty for specified crimes. . . . The Fifth Amendment, adopted at the same time as the Eighth, contemplated the continued existence of the capital sanction by imposing certain limits on the prosecution of capital cases. . . . And the Fourteenth Amendment, adopted over three-quarters of a century later, similarly contemplates the existence of the capital sanction in providing that no State shall deprive any person of "life, liberty, or property" without due process of law. . . .

. . . Despite the continuing debate, dating back to the 19th century, over the morality and utility of capital punishment, it is now evident that a large proportion of American society continues to regard it as an appropriate and necessary criminal sanction. . . .

Finally, we must consider whether the punishment of death is disproportionate in relation to the crime for which it is imposed. . . . when a life has been taken deliberately by the offender, we cannot say that the punishment is invariably disproportionate to the crime. It is an extreme sanction, suitable to the most extreme of crimes. . . .

. . . the concerns expressed in *Furman* that the penalty of death not be imposed in an arbitrary or capricious manner can be met by a carefully drafted statute that ensures that the sentencing authority is given adequate information and guidance.

Source: Gregg v. Georgia, 428 U.S. 153 (1976).

Remarks by U.S. President George W. Bush at the Signing of the USA PATRIOT Act, October 26, 2001

Within two months after the terrorist attacks on the United States on September 11, 2001, the U.S. Congress quickly passed the USA PATRIOT Act. The act's title is short for "Uniting and Strengthening America by Providing Appropriate Tools Required to Intercept and Obstruct Terrorism." U.S. president George W. Bush signed the act into law two days later. In order to prevent future terrorist attacks, the act greatly increased the power of the federal government to secretly watch, listen in on, and track communications (such as telephone calls, voice mail, and e-mail), to control the actions of banks and other financial institutions, to hold and deport immigrants suspected of being terrorists, and to prevent foreign terrorists from entering the country. The act also made some crimes (such as terrorist attacks on buses, trains, or other forms of mass transportation) federal crimes for the first time, increased the punishment for many federal crimes, and increased the statute of limitations for crimes of terrorism. Several sections of the act that relate to foreign intelligence and domestic spying will end on

December 31, 2005, unless Congress renews these sections. Below are excerpts from President Bush's remarks at his signing of the USA PATRIOT Act.

Good morning and welcome to the White House. Today, we take an essential step in defeating terrorism, while protecting the constitutional rights of all Americans. With my signature, this law will give intelligence and law enforcement officials important new tools to fight a present danger. . . .

The changes, effective today, will help counter a threat like no other our nation has ever faced. We've seen the enemy, and the murder of thousands of innocent, unsuspecting people. They recognize no barrier of morality. They have no conscience. The terrorists cannot be reasoned with. Witness the recent anthrax attacks through our Postal Service. . . .

But one thing is for certain: These terrorists must be pursued, they must be defeated, and they must be brought to justice. And that is the purpose of this legislation. . . .

. . . We're dealing with terrorists who operate by highly sophisticated methods and technologies, some of which were not even available when our existing laws were written. The bill before me takes account of the new realities and dangers posed by modern terrorists. It will help law enforcement to identify, to dismantle, to disrupt, and to punish terrorists before they strike.

For example, this legislation gives law enforcement officials better tools to put an end to financial counterfeiting, smuggling and money-laundering. Secondly, it gives intelligence operations and criminal operations the chance to operate not on separate tracks, but to share vital information so necessary to disrupt a terrorist attack before it occurs.

As of today, we're changing the laws governing information-sharing. And as importantly, we're changing the culture of our various agencies that fight terrorism. Countering and investigating terrorist activity is the number one priority for both law enforcement and intelligence agencies.

Surveillance of communications is another essential tool to pursue and stop terrorists. The existing law was written in the era of rotary telephones. This new law that I sign today will allow surveillance of all communications used by terrorists, including e-mails, the Internet, and cell phones.

As of today, we'll be able to better meet the technological challenges posed by this proliferation of communications technology. Investigations are often slowed by limit on the reach of federal search warrants.

Law enforcement agencies have to get a new warrant for each new district they investigate, even when they're after the same suspect. Under this new law, warrants are valid across all districts and across all states. And, finally, the new legislation greatly enhances the penalties that will fall on terrorists or anyone who helps them.

Current statutes deal more severely with drug-traffickers than with terrorists. That changes today. We are enacting new and harsh penalties for possession of biological weapons. We're making it easier to seize the assets of groups and individuals involved in terrorism. The government will have wider latitude in deporting known terrorists and their supporters. The statute of limitations on terrorist acts will be lengthened, as will prison sentences for terrorists.

. . . This bill met with an overwhelming—overwhelming agreement in Congress, because it upholds and respects the civil liberties guaranteed by our Constitution.

This legislation is essential not only to pursuing and punishing terrorists, but also preventing more atrocities in the hands of the evil ones. This government will enforce this law with all the urgency of a nation at war. The elected branches of our government, and both political parties, are united in our resolve to fight and stop and punish those who would do harm to the American people.

It is now my honor to sign into law the USA Patriot Act of 2001.

Source: The White House, "President Signs Anti-Terrorism Bill: Remarks by the President at Signing of the Patriot Act, Anti-Terrorism Legislation," The White House. Available online. URL: http://www.whitehouse.gov/news/releases/ 2001/10/20011026-5.html. Downloaded on November 26, 2004.

Rasul v. Bush, June 28, 2004

On October 7, 2001, the United States and its ally Great Britain began a war against Afghanistan, the country harboring al-Qaeda, the terrorist group that planned the attacks against the United States on September 11, 2001. In December, the United States and military allies drove the Taliban from power. During the war in Afghanistan, the United States captured or killed thousands of Islamic militants. After the war, the United States transferred enemy fighters who were not U.S. citizens to the country's naval base at Guantánamo Bay, Cuba.

U.S. president George W. Bush declared that the prisoners at Guantánamo Bay are not prisoners of war, but unlawful enemy combatants; therefore, he claimed, they do not have the same rights as traditional prisoners of war, such as the right not to be tortured. The Bush administration also denied that the prisoners at Guantánamo had the right of habeas corpus. In *Rasul v. Bush,* the U.S. Supreme Court said that the prisoners at Guantánamo do have this right. Shafiq Rasul, the petitioner named in the case, had been released by the time the Court delivered its opinion. Along with *Rasul,* the Court also heard *Al Odah v. United States.* Below are excerpts from the Court opinion in *Rasul.*

JUSTICE STEVENS delivered the opinion of the Court.

These two cases [*Rasul v. Bush* and *Al Odah v. United States*] present the narrow but important question whether United States courts lack jurisdiction to consider challenges to the legality of the detention of foreign nationals captured abroad in connection with hostilities and incarcerated at the Guantánamo Bay Naval Base, Cuba. . . .

Respondents' primary submission is that the answer to the jurisdictional question is controlled by our decision in [*Johnson v.*] *Eisentrager* [(1950)]. In that case, we held that a Federal District Court lacked authority to issue a writ of habeas corpus to 21 German citizens who had been captured by U.S. forces in China, tried and convicted of war crimes by an American military commission headquartered in Nanking, and incarcerated in the Landsberg Prison in occupied Germany. . . .

Petitioners in these cases differ from the *Eisentrager* detainees in important respects: They are not nationals of countries at war with the United States, and they deny that they have engaged in or plotted acts of aggression against the United States; they have never been afforded access to any tribunal, much less charged with and convicted of wrongdoing; and for more than two years they have been imprisoned in territory over which the United States exercises exclusive jurisdiction and control. . . .

. . . In *Braden v. 30th Judicial Circuit Court of Ky.,* 410 U.S. 484, 495 (1973), this Court held . . . that the prisoner's presence within the territorial jurisdiction of the district court is not "an invariable prerequisite" to the exercise of district court jurisdiction under the federal habeas statute. Rather, because "the writ of habeas corpus does not act upon the prisoner who seeks relief, but upon the person who holds him in what is alleged to be unlawful custody," a district court acts "within [its] respective jurisdiction" within the meaning of [section] 2241 [of the federal habeas corpus statute (28 U.S.C. 2241)] as long as "the custodian can be reached by service of process". . . .

. . . respondents contend that we can discern a limit on §2241 through application of the "longstanding principle of American law" that congressional legislation is presumed not to have extraterritorial application unless such intent is clearly manifested. . . . Whatever traction the presumption against extraterritoriality might have in other contexts, it certainly has no application to the operation of the habeas statute with respect to persons detained within "the territorial jurisdiction" of the United States. . . . By the express terms of its agreements with Cuba, the United States exercises "complete jurisdiction and control" over the Guantánamo Bay Naval Base, and may continue to exercise such control permanently if it so chooses. . . . Considering that the statute draws no distinction between Americans and aliens held in federal custody, there is little reason to think that Congress intended the geographical coverage of the statute to vary depending on the detainee's citizenship. Aliens held at the base, no less than American citizens, are entitled to invoke the federal courts' authority under §2241. . . .

In the end, the answer to the question presented is clear. Petitioners contend that they are being held in federal custody in violation of the laws of the United States. No party questions the District Court's jurisdiction over petitioners' custodians. . . . Section 2241, by its terms, requires nothing more. We therefore hold that §2241 confers on the District Court jurisdiction to hear petitioners' habeas corpus challenges to the legality of their detention at the Guantánamo Bay Naval Base.

Source: Rasul v. Bush, No. 03-334 (U.S. June 28, 2004).

Hamdi v. Rumsfeld, June 28, 2004

During the war against Afghanistan after the September 11 attacks, the government seized U.S. citizens who were connected with the Taliban. After the war, the U.S. government transferred these citizens to the United States and held them as "enemy combatants." In *Hamdi,* the federal government argued that it had the right to hold citizens as enemy combatants without charging them or putting them on trial. The government also argued that U.S. courts had no power to review a decision by the military that a citizen is an enemy combatant. The Court agreed that the government has the power to hold U.S. citizens as enemy combatants. The Court, however, also declared that the prisoners have the right to challenge their imprisonment in court.

On October 11, 2004, the U.S. government freed Hamdi on the conditions that he give up his U.S. citizenship, renounce terrorism, and live in Saudi Arabia for five years. Hamdi's agreement with the United States also bars him from traveling to Afghanistan, Iraq, Israel, Syria, the West Bank (territory occupied by Israel), and the Gaza Strip (a region adjoining Egypt and Israel). The agreement also requires that he not sue the U.S. government for holding him and that he notify officials in Saudi Arabia if he finds out about "any planned or executed acts of terrorism." Below are excerpts from the Court opinion in *Hamdi.*

JUSTICE O'CONNOR announced the judgment of the Court and delivered an opinion, in which THE CHIEF JUSTICE, JUSTICE KENNEDY, and JUSTICE BREYER join.

At this difficult time in our Nation's history, we are called upon to consider the legality of the Government's detention of a United States citizen on United States soil as an "enemy combatant" and to address the process that is constitutionally owed to one who seeks to challenge his classification as such. . . . We hold that although Congress authorized the detention of combatants in the narrow circumstances alleged here, due process demands that a citizen held in the United States as an enemy combatant be given a meaningful opportunity to contest the factual basis for that detention before a neutral decisionmaker. . . .

In so holding, we necessarily reject the Government's assertion that separation of powers principles mandate a heavily circumscribed role for the courts in such circumstances. . . . We have long since made clear that a state of war is not a blank check for the President when it comes to the rights of the Nation's citizens. . . . Whatever power the United States Constitution envisions for the Executive in its exchanges with other nations or with enemy organizations in times of conflict, it most assuredly envisions a role for all three branches when individual liberties are at stake.

Source: Hamdi v. Rumsfeld, No. 03-6696 (U.S. June 28, 2004).

Further Reading

Berger, Leslie. *The Grand Jury*. Crime, Justice, and Punishment, edited by Austin Sarat. Philadelphia: Chelsea House, 2000.

Campbell, Andrea. *Rights of the Accused*. Crime, Justice, and Punishment, edited by Austin Sarat. Philadelphia: Chelsea House, 2001.

Day, Nancy. *The Death Penalty for Teens: A Pro/Con Issue*. Hot Pro/Con Issues. Berkeley Heights, N.J.: Enslow, 2000.

Dudley, Mark E. *Gideon v. Wainwright (1963): Right to Counsel*. Supreme Court Decisions. New York: Twenty-First Century Books, 1995.

Fireside, Harvey. *The Fifth Amendment: The Right to Remain Silent*. Constitution. Springfield, N.J.: Enslow, 1998.

Freedman, Russell. *In Defense of Liberty: The Story of America's Bill of Rights*. New York: Holiday House, 2003.

Gold, Susan Dudley. *Miranda v. Arizona (1966): Suspects' Rights*. Supreme Court Decisions. New York: Twenty-First Century Books, 1995.

Gottfried, Ted. *Capital Punishment: The Death Penalty Debate*. Issues in Focus. Springfield, N.J.: Enslow, 1997.

———. *Homeland Security versus Constitutional Rights*. Brookfield, Conn.: Twenty-First Century Books, 2003.

Herda, D. J. *Furman v. Georgia: The Death Penalty Case*. Landmark Supreme Court Cases. Hillside, N.J.: Enslow, 1994.

Marzilli, Alan. *Capital Punishment*. Point-Counterpoint. Philadelphia: Chelsea House, 2003.

Persico, Deborah A. *Mapp v. Ohio: Evidence and Search Warrants*. Landmark Supreme Court Cases. Springfield, N.J.: Enslow, 1997.

Pettifor, Bonnie, and Charles E. Petit. *Weeks v. United States: Illegal Search and Seizure*. Landmark Supreme Court Cases. Berkeley Heights, N.J.: Enslow, 2000.

Ramen, Fred. *The Right to Freedom from Searches*. Individual Rights and Civic Responsibility. New York: Rosen Publishing Group, 2001.

———. *The Rights of the Accused*. Individual Rights and Civil Responsibility. New York: Rosen Publishing Group, 2001.

Riley, Gail Blasser. *Miranda v. Arizona: Rights of the Accused*. Landmark Supreme Court Cases. Hillside, N.J.: Enslow, 1994.

Sherrow, Victoria. *Gideon v. Wainwright: Free Legal Counsel*. Landmark Supreme Court Cases. Springfield, N.J.: Enslow, 1995.

Wetterer, Charles M. *The Fourth Amendment: Search and Seizure*. Constitution. Springfield, N.J.: Enslow, 1998.

Wice, Paul B. *Miranda v. Arizona: "You Have the Right To Remain Silent. . . ."* New York: Franklin Watts, 1996.

Williams, Mary E., ed. *The Death Penalty*. Opposing Viewpoints Series. San Diego, Calif.: Greenhaven, 2002.

Wolf, Robert V. *Capital Punishment*. Crime, Justice, and Punishment, edited by Austin Sarat. Philadelphia: Chelsea House, 1997.

———. *The Jury System*. Crime, Justice, and Punishment, edited by Austin Sarat. Philadelphia: Chelsea House, 1997.

Bibliography

General Adult Sources

Bedau, Hugo Adam, ed. *The Death Penalty in America*. 3d ed. New York: Oxford University Press, 1982.

———. *The Death Penalty in America: Current Controversies*. New York: Oxford University Press, 1997.

Bodenhamer, David J. *Fair Trial: Rights of the Accused in American History*. New York: Oxford University Press, 1992.

Bowers, William J. *Legal Homicide: Death as Punishment in America, 1864–1982*. Rev. ed. of *Executions in America*. 1974. Boston: Northeastern University Press, 1984.

Cogan, Neil H., ed. *The Complete Bill of Rights: The Drafts, Debates, Sources, and Origins*. New York: Oxford University Press, 1997.

Cuddihy, William, and B. Carmon Hardy. "A Man's House Was Not His Castle: Origins of the Fourth Amendment to the United States Constitution." *William and Mary Quarterly* 37, no. 3 (1980): pp. 371–400.

Doyle, Charles. *Terrorism: Section by Section Analysis of the USA PATRIOT Act*. Updated December 10, 2001. CRS Report for Congress. Order code RL31200. Washington, D.C.: Congressional Research Service, Library of Congress, 2001. Also available through the Internet from the Electronic Privacy Information Center Web site. URL: http://www.epic.org/privacy/terrorism/usapatriot/. Updated on July 29, 2004.

———. *The USA PATRIOT Act: A Legal Analysis*. April 15, 2002. CRS Report for Congress. Order code RL31377. [Washington, D.C.]: Congressional Research Service, Library of Congress, 2002. Also available through the Internet from the Electronic Privacy Information Center Web site. URL: http://www.epic.org/privacy/terrorism/usapatriot/. Updated on July 29, 2004. Also available through the Internet from the Federation of American Scientists Web site. URL: http://fas.org/irp/crs/. Updated on July 19, 2004.

———. *USA PATRIOT Act Sunset: Provisions That Expire on December 31, 2005.* Updated June 20, 2004. CRS Report for Congress. Order code RL32186. [Washington, D.C.]: Congressional Research Service, Library of Congress, 2004. Also available through the Internet from the Federation of American Scientists Web site. URL: http://fas.org/irp/crs/. Updated on July 19, 2004.

Gregg, Pauline. *Free-Born John: A Biography of John Lilburne.* London: Harrap, 1961.

Griffith, Robert. *The Politics of Fear: Joseph R. McCarthy and the Senate.* 2d ed. Amherst: University of Massachusetts Press, 1987.

Howard, A. E. Dick. *The Road from Runnymede: Magna Carta and Constitutionalism in America.* Virginia Legal Studies. Charlottesville: University of Virginia Press, 1968.

Lasson, Nelson B. *The History and Development of the Fourth Amendment to the United States Constitution.* The Johns Hopkins University Studies in Historical and Political Science, series LV, no. 2. Baltimore: Johns Hopkins University Press, 1937.

Levy, Leonard W. *Against the Law: The Nixon Court and Criminal Justice.* New York: Harper and Row, 1974.

———. *Origins of the Bill of Rights.* New Haven, Conn.: Yale University Press, 1999.

———. *Origins of the Fifth Amendment: The Right against Self-Incrimination.* New York: Oxford University Press, 1968. Reprint, with a new preface, New York: Macmillan, 1986.

———. *The Palladium of Justice: Origins of Trial by Jury.* Chicago: Ivan R. Dee, 1999.

Levy, Leonard W., and Kenneth L. Karst, eds. *Encyclopedia of the American Constitution.* 2d ed. 6 vols. New York: Macmillan Reference USA, 2000.

Lewis, Anthony. *Gideon's Trumpet.* New York: Random House, 1964.

National Commission on Terrorist Attacks upon the United States. *The 9/11 Commission Report: Final Report of the National Commission on Terrorist Attacks upon the United States.* Official government ed. Washington, D.C.: National Commission on Terrorist Attacks upon the United States, 2004. Also available through the Internet from the GPO Access Web site. URL: http://www.gpoaccess.gov/911/index.html. Updated on July 29, 2004.

Oshinsky, David M. *A Conspiracy So Immense: The World of Joe McCarthy.* New York: Free Press, 1983.

Plucknett, Theodore F. T. *A Concise History of the Common Law.* 5th ed. Boston: Little, Brown, 1956.

Rutland, Robert Allen. *The Birth of the Bill of Rights, 1776–1791.* Bicentennial ed. Boston: Northeastern University Press, 1991.

Schrecker, Ellen. *Many Are the Crimes: McCarthyism in America.* Boston: Little, Brown, 1998.

Schwartz, Bernard, comp. *Roots of the Bill of Rights.* 5 vols. New York: Chelsea House, 1980.

Thomas, George C., III. *Double Jeopardy: The History, the Law.* New York: New York University Press, 1998.

United States. *The Constitution of the United States of America: Analysis and Interpretation: 2000 Supplement: Analysis of Cases Decided by the Supreme Court of the United States to June 28, 2000.* Edited by George A. Costello and Kenneth R. Thomas. 106th Cong., 2nd sess., 2000. S. Doc. 27. Also available through the Internet from the GPO Access Web site. URL: http://www.gpoaccess.gov/constitution/index.html. Updated on July 15, 2004.

———. *The Constitution of the United States of America: Analysis and Interpretation: Annotations of Cases Decided by the Supreme Court of the United States to June 29, 1992.* Prepared by the Congressional Research Service, Library of Congress. Edited by Johnny H. Killian and George A. Costello. 103rd Cong., 1st sess., 1996. S. Doc. 6. Also available through the Internet from the GPO Access Web site. URL: http://www.gpoaccess.gov/constitution/index.html. Updated on July 15, 2004. Web version also available at the FindLaw Web site. URL: http://www.findlaw.com/casecode/constitution/. Downloaded on July 25, 2004. The Web version also includes the information from the 1996, 1998, and 2000 supplements.

U.S. Congress. Senate Select Committee to Study Governmental Operations with Respect to Intelligence Activities. *Final Report of the Select Committee to Study Governmental Operations with Respect to Intelligence Activities, United States Senate: Together with Additional, Supplemental, and Separate Views.* 6 vols. 94th Cong., 2d sess., 1976. S. Rept. 755.

U.S. Department of Justice. Bureau of Justice Statistics. *Capital Punishment, 2003*. November 2004. Also available through the Internet from the Bureau of Justice Statistics Web site. URL: http://www.ojp.usdoj.gov/bjs/abstract/cp03htm. Downloaded on November 21, 2004.

U.S. National Archives and Records Administration. "Magna Carta and Its American Legacy." U.S. National Archives and Records Administration. Available online. URL: http://www.archives.gov/exhibit_hall/featured_documents/magna_carta/legacy.html. Downloaded on July 30, 2004.

———. "A More Perfect Union: The Creation of the U.S. Constitution." U.S. National Archives and Records Administration. Available online. URL: http://www.archives.gov/national_archives_experience/charters/constitution_history.html. Downloaded on July 24, 2004. Based on Bruns, Roger A. Introduction to *A More Perfect Union: The Creation of the United States Constitution*. Washington, D.C.: National Archives Trust Fund Board, 1986.

Online Document Collections

Cornell Law School. Legal Information Institute. Supreme Court Collection. URL: http://supct.law.cornell.edu/supct/. Downloaded on July 31, 2004.

FindLaw. Cases and Codes. URL: http://www.findlaw.com/casecode/. Downloaded on July 31, 2004.

U.S. National Archives and Records Administration. The Charters of Freedom. URL: http://www.archives.gov/national_archives_experience/charters/charters.html. Downloaded on July 31, 2004.

Yale Law School. The Avalon Project at Yale Law School: Documents in Law, History, and Diplomacy. URL: http://www.yale.edu/lawweb/avalon/avalon.htm. Downloaded on July 25, 2004.

Index

Page numbers in *italic* indicate photographs. Page numbers in **boldface** indicate box features and margin quotations. Page numbers followed by *m* indicate maps. Page numbers followed by *t* indicate tables or graphs. Page numbers followed by *g* indicate glossary entries. Page numbers followed by *c* indicate chronology entries.